# Sparkle Kitty

## Embracing a Child's Wisdom

By William A. Howatt, Ph.D.

A Way With Words Editorial Services

Copyright © 2001 by A Way With Words Editorial Services. All rights reserved. No part of this book may be reproduced, stored in a retrieval system, or transcribed in any form or by any means – electronic, mechanical, photocopying, recording or otherwise – without the prior written permission of the publisher.

Printed in Nova Scotia, Canada

10 9 8 7 6 5 4 3 2 1

ISBN 1-894338-35-9

Published 2001

Edited by Anna-Maria Galante-Ward
Cover by Joan Sinclair Design
Sparkle Kitty illustration by Emily Howatt, a.k.a. Sparkle Kitty
Glasser's Choice Behaviour Chart graphic by Don Crowell

A Way With Words Editorial Services
83 Apple Tree Lane
Kentville NS B4N 5C1

# Table of Contents

**Introduction: A Change of Heart** .......................... 5
   Sparkle Kitty's Nine "Childmind" Principles ............ 9

**Section 1:** ................................................. 13
  **Chapter 1: The Power of Love** ........................ 13
    Ten Tips to Increase Your Love for Others ........... 21
    Sparkle Action ...................................... 23
  **Chapter 2: The Power of Courage** ..................... 25
    Sparkle Kitty's Decision Model ...................... 28
    Ten Tips to Develop Courage ......................... 29
    Glasser's Choice Behaviour Chart .................... 34
    Sparkle Action ...................................... 36
  **Chapter 3: The Power of Fun** ......................... 37
    Ten Tips to Add Fun and Recreation .................. 43
    Sparkle Action ...................................... 45

**Section 2: The Power of Open Mind** ....................... 47
  **Chapter 4: The Power of Hope** ........................ 47
    The Power of Positive Thinking ...................... 48
    The Power of Language ............................... 51
    Self-Acceptance is a Skill;
       Self-Esteem is the Habit of Using It ........... 52
    Tips for Building Self-Acceptance ................... 54
    Tips for Enhancing Self-Esteem ...................... 55
    Self-Affirmation .................................... 56
    What Is Your Personality? ........................... 57
    Twenty Personality Traits That Help People
       Think Positively ............................... 57
    Is Image a Booster or a Buster? ..................... 60
    Tips for Creating Positive Thinking ................. 63
    Sparkle Action ...................................... 66
  **Chapter 5: The Power of Imagination** ................. 67
    Overcoming Life Potholes ............................ 71
    A Guide to Solving Life Potholes .................... 73
    Ten Tips to Increase your Creativity ................ 74
    Sparkle Action ...................................... 76

## Chapter 6: The Power of Learning ....... 77
- Technological Versus Psychological Growth ........ 80
- Help is Available ........ 87
- Tips to Improve your Life Learning ........ 87
- Sparkle Action ........ 89

# Section 3: The Power of Open Soul ........ 91

## Chapter 7: The Power of Faith ........ 91
- Why Have Faith? ........ 94
- Overcoming Character Flaws and Bad Karma ........ 97
- Ten Tips to Add Faith to Your Life ........ 98
- Sparkle Action ........ 101

## Chapter 8: The Power of Family and Relationships ........ 101
- Relationships Are Challenging – But We Need Them ........ 108
- Improving Communication Skills ........ 108
- Techniques for Building Rapport ........ 109
- Ten Tips for Building Your Family and Relationships ........ 113
- Sparkle Action ........ 116

## Chapter 9: The Power of Dreams ........ 117
- The Path of Turning Dreams into Reality ........ 118
- Defining Your Dream ........ 122
- Ten Tips to Help Your Dreams Come True ........ 124
- Sparkle Action ........ 126

# Final Thoughts ........ 127

# Appendix A: Your Childmind Score ........ 129

# References ........ 135

# Introduction

## A Change of Heart

REGARDLESS of the day or time, if you ask Emily Howatt, a.k.a. Sparkle Kitty, how she is, she will say, "Just great!"

And it remains a miracle for my wife and me.

Emily was only a few hours old the first time she momentarily stopped breathing. It was almost two weeks later before we found out there was something wrong with her heart. She was a month premature, and although my wife Sherrie had had a good labour, there were complications following the delivery, and Sherrie had to go into surgery when Emily was just a few minutes old.

By her side throughout the labour and delivery, I had seen Sherrie lose a lot of blood. Then she was whisked into another room, and I was terrified she might not come back. There I sat, alone with my new baby girl, and I realized I didn't know a thing.

I was grateful beyond words when Sherrie finally got to hold Emily a few hours later. And the next day, when Emily cried, Sherrie got out of bed for the first time to pick her up. They watched the sunrise together, and Sherrie told her she would never have to be afraid.

Then all hell broke loose, and we were all afraid.

We soon learned Emily's lungs were compromised because the walls inside her heart hadn't formed completely. She was going to need substantial open-heart surgery. The family doctor told us she wouldn't live longer than two years without the operation, and that a cold or flu in the next six months could put her life at risk.

Sherrie hung a sign on the door of our house, warning visitors with the sniffles not to even bother to knock. She breastfed Emily for about five months, and got her straight through to her surgery cold-free – despite the surgery date being cancelled twice.

Sherrie also had to make some career choices in that time. She had been running a very successful Hallmark Gold Crown gift shop up until Emily's birth, and she had been voted Kings County's businessperson of the year. But ultimately she chose to devote herself to Emily's wellness.

Finally, we had a firm surgery date on November 17. Neither one of us could bring ourselves to even think about Christmas.

The operation would require something more than a "simple" patch – it would require what the doctors considered a reconstruction of "medium" difficulty. Sherrie now knows of another child who had a "simple" patch, who died after developing an infection.

We were apprehensive about just getting through the day, knowing Emily's little eight-month-old body would be cooled down for the duration of the surgery – and that she'd be technically dead for those six hours, connected to a heart-lung machine at the Izaak Walton Killam Children's Hospital in Halifax. After the operation, they would raise her body temperature until her heart started up again on its own.

Sherrie was beside herself with anxiety. She pinned a note to Emily's diaper for the surgeon, to try to give Emily some identity. It said, "Good morning, my name is Emily. My Mommy and Daddy are scared to death. Please take good care of me."

The night before, we were sleepless, wondering if the surgical team was getting a good night's sleep, but knowing we had no control over them. We had to trust, completely.

That trust was not in vain. The operation was successful. Needless to say, Sherrie and I are eternally indebted to Dr. David Ross. Two weeks after the surgery, we were back in Halifax for Emily's follow-up, and we finally had the doctor's permission to take her out in public. We'd had a private baptism for her in our hometown of Kentville, at the United Church of St. Paul and St. Stephen.

Sherrie hadn't bought a single Christmas present. She wouldn't even allow herself to think about a first birthday, a party. She didn't even go shopping until weeks after that first surgery. Only then did she believe Emily would turn one, and that we would get to see her grow up.

If you have ever had a sick child, you know how quickly their health becomes your priority. If you have ever faced the loss of a child, you know it impacts every level of your being. I believe Emily's illness forced me to focus on her in a way I likely wouldn't have had she been well. God works in mysterious ways.

Her illness woke me up! I was suddenly a very captive audience. I was shown what all children have to offer to us adults about life. All we need is strong enough motivation to listen to them. We can learn a great deal from our children if we recognize just how lucky we are to be in their presence.

You do not need to have children to get the message – or understand this book. Watch the children around you. Emily's surgery left me with no choice. From the day she was born, she was under a microscope, and I prayed to God that I would never lose her. To this day I pray. A life crisis will teach you to notice the things that are important to you. *PLEASE DON'T WAIT FOR A LIFE CRISIS TO WAKE YOU UP.*

As a person, I was reborn observing my daughter. It also made me a good parent. It's clear to me that Emily already lives life with wisdom. Now that I have been paying attention, I know I was not fully incorporating my own wisdom into my life. It's been said the child is the father of the man. Many of us don't grow up until we have a child in our lives. Until that point, many of us have never had to venture beyond our own ego-needs.

Jon Kabat-Zinn (1995) has written that "a baby is a live-in Zen master," meaning an infant's cries and basic demands alone will quickly separate you from your attachments and delusions – true enough of any baby. And babies *do* have a certain bald-headed, Buddha-like grace; especially once they've learned to sit contented.

Korean Zen master Seung Sahn (1997) said, "Child's mind is Buddha's mind. Just seeing, just doing is truth. Then, using this mind means when you are hungry, eat. When someone is hungry, give them food."

But there is even more to the saving grace of a child than all the practical changes it will effect in your life. The love of a child is unconditional, and returning it is transformational.

The parent-child relationship is the basis for many Judaeo-Christian metaphors, and the Bible is replete with references to children. Consider Christ's message in three of the four gospels:

"Truly I tell you, unless you change and become like children, you will never enter the kingdom of heaven. Whoever becomes humble like this child is the greatest in the kingdom of heaven. Whoever welcomes one such child in my name welcomes me." (Matthew 18:1-5)

When we learn to love a child, we learn to love like a child too, and that can be a key to great personal fulfilment. So here is the kingdom – here and now – within grasp of all of us, and accessible to a child.

In the Old Testament, the prophet Isaiah foresees a coming time of peace in which

"The wolf shall live with the lamb, the leopard shall lie down with the kid, the calf and the lion and the fatling together, and a little child shall lead them." (Isaiah 11:6)

The "peaceable kingdom" is something we as a society and nation are capable of creating now – both within and amongst ourselves – if we can remember the priorities we had as young children, before we became competitive in our looks, chequebooks, and intellectual accomplishments.

We aren't going to fulfil our potential, or became better people in any meaningful sense, unless we employ some civility in our day-to-day life.

This book is based on nine life principles I have drawn from observation. These are ideas boiled down from seven years of parenting a child who is both very special, and at the same time, *everychild*. The interesting and ironic truth is that we all started out life with the "childmind" attributes listed below. Without question we all need them to live our lives to the full. If you take these principles to heart, and develop them in your daily life, they will lead you to new habits of living that will benefit you and the world around you. For along with an open heart, open mind, and open soul, come civility, morality, and law-abiding citizenship.

Once you've incorporated the childmind habits, you'll find yourself more able to enjoy each day, clearer on the meaning of life, and how to live it.

Emily created the name Sparkle Kitty to represent her power over herself and her life. Being a sick child, her imagination developed this character to help provide her with the resolve to live life to the fullest. In my son Tommy's case (age 4), he has an "Uncle Worgee." The point is that all children have the programming on board to run the following nine life principles. What they need is the support, modelling, and permission to turn these programs into life-long habits.

## *Sparkle Kitty's Nine "Childmind" Principles*

**Power of Open Heart**

1. Love – "I love Everybody!"
2. Courage – "I can DO it."
3. Fun – "It's your turn to play with me."

**Power of Open Mind**

4. Hope – "They're going to just love me."
5. Imagination – "Little Rosie is here."
6. Learning – "Can I ask you a question?"

**Power of Open Soul**

7. Faith – "I am thankful for God."
8. Family – "I love Howatts."
9. Dreams – "I'm going to fix hearts some day."

With age, a large portion of the population has forgotten these ways of being. Emily has the wisdom that all children are born with. I believe we are all born perfectly equipped for the job ahead of us. I also believe we never entirely lose these nine basic values. However, the path we choose through life inevitably influences the way we define our experience and create our realities. As the Jedi master Qui-Gonn advises his young charge in the first episode of the Star Wars movies: "Your focus is your reality."

Many of us forget what is really important as we mature into adults. A large section of the population between the ages of 7 and 77 is in turmoil. Unfortunately, many of us spend our youth and prime searching for answers, and struggling to enjoy life. Happiness is difficult without life balance, and life balance is difficult unless you can juggle the demands of money, career, relationships, self, and health. In balance, these five are sources of happiness; out of balance, they are stressors, as borne out by the following:

1. If it is true that 95 percent of the wealth is controlled by 5 percent of the population, then a large portion of the population is worried about money.

2. If it is true that 60 percent of working people do not like their jobs, career satisfaction is a major preoccupation.
3. If it is true that 70 percent of all marriages end in separation or divorce, our relationship skills need work.
4. If it is true that 80 percent of people place great importance on the opinions of others, our self-worth is in jeopardy.
5. If it is true that 90 percent of people do not have a healthy attitude about fitness and physical wellness, we need to learn how to have fun all over again.

Where is our society heading? Is it living by solid principles and civility? I believe it is off course in this regard. If, as I believe, we are all born with the answers for living, using strong civility principles, all we need is to be reminded of them. Why have we, as a society, forgotten? Our civility, our lack of it, hinges on our values. Don't our values demand more than lip service? Perhaps the truth is that many members of our society are out of balance because they are not living life by solid principles. The childmind principles are a simple access to life balance. The goal of this book is to prompt you to *stop and remember what you already know.*

Each chapter of this book has been written to provide you with ideas and suggestions on incorporating each childmind principle into your life. This book is a guide, to increase your awareness. If it does that, and helps you to a new beginning, it has achieved its objective. The journey of life offers many lessons. My baby Emily influenced me - let's see if she does you as well.

I have been in the field of counselling, teaching, and consulting for the past sixteen years. In that time, one of the chief conclusions I have reached about people is that we complicate our own lives. One of the most common misconceptions is thinking someone else will fix things. A significant cross-section of the population does not see that they have the power to improve their own world. If we only live once, we need to do *our* best - not somebody else's.

When I started counselling, I quickly made the assumption that I was fine, happy and balanced enough to help others. I threw myself into the role of repairman and expert. I was confident in my training, and believed that once I started making money and established a good career, life would start for me. Once I climbed that mountain I could relax and enjoy life.

# INTRODUCTION

Emily has reminded me of how I had missed the boat. The fact was, I was always living life. I just had excuses for not enjoying it. I was like the plumber with leaky taps in his own kitchen, the auto body specialist who drives a rusty car. I was helping others live their lives, and forgetting to live mine. I can tell you my ego was the first issue I needed to overcome. It was hard for me to accept the fact I was not doing what I was preaching.

My awakening showed me I was not living my life with a balanced mind. My focus was career and money. I was missing my relationships, self and health. As I think back, I had a good income, worked extremely hard, and enjoyed my career, but not my life. My dreams of the white picket fence and happy family were drifting, because I was obsessed with my career and money. I was not enjoying life moment by moment. I was only able to enjoy life if my career and bank account would allow me. Can you relate to this?

One of the main reasons people chase money and material things is the mistaken perception that they will derive emotional gain from having more. Once our survival needs are met, all other wants are really for perceived emotional gain. Does more money buy happiness? The answer is no! For me, the biggest hang-up was not allowing myself to enjoy life - or say it was *just great* - until I had more money and a great career. And no, more money was never enough!

Some people say they are too busy to enjoy life. They are too busy looking for shortcuts when the fact is there is none. There are no shortcuts to living with values. The path to civility lies in each one of us practicing our virtues – to use an old-fashioned word.

As you review the childmind principles, consider your own values, and how well you are keeping them. Four revealing questions to help you take a quick life inventory are:

1. Where are you now in your life?
2. Where do you want to go?
3. What do you need so you can do it?
4. Are you willing to do what it takes?

Childmind will work only if you are willing to do what it takes to make it a reality. Don't, however, be discouraged. In my research, it takes, on average, 12 to 18 months for a new habit to become ingrained. We need to route a behaviour 600 to 700 times before it becomes an automatic habit. Approach the nine childmind principles the same way. It's a lifelong journey. I'm still recovering the overgrown path back to my childmind.

Religious wars, hunger, crime and drugs are all signs that our world is not the best it could be. What would the world be like if a five-year-old were in charge? If we have created these problems, there is hope we can solve them. But we can't solve problems on the level of thinking that created them, as Einstein pointed out. So we all need to start with ourselves for our society to increase civility as a whole.

Best wishes,

Sparkle Kitty's Dad,
Sparkle Fox

Kentville, Nova Scotia, November 2001

Section 1:

# Chapter 1

# The Power of Love

*"I love Everybody!" – Sparkle Kitty*

"Daddy!"

"Yes, Emily?"

"Daddy, I love you!"

Every time I hear these words, my heart grows warm, and water appears in my eyes. I can tell you that I did not ever think I could love the way I do. It was not until my daughter came into my life did I see and understand the power of love. I love my parents and my wife, but Sparkle Kitty has ignited a flame of an intensity I did not foresee. At first, I was afraid I would never love any of my future children the way I do Sparkle Kitty. But I have also learned that there is more love in me than I ever thought possible. The experience of being a parent has taught me what unconditional love is.

Sparkle Kitty reintroduced me to love. She has a great deal of love for people close to her, and loves to be with new people. She has such a passion for everyone and everything. She has empathy for every creature – even squished ants.

Sparkle Kitty teaches me that we need to be kind to everyone and everything. What kind of world would it be if everyone was able to love in this open, childlike way? This kind of love is the basis for the New Testament, but Christianity isn't the only religion centered on compassion.

Where does love come from? What influences us to build love into our lives? Human beings need to balance material and spiritual, self and other. We all need food, shelter and clothing to survive, and a source of income by which these needs can be met, usually a career. We need to like who we are, and without health, our efforts won't last long. But besides all of this, we need to have at least one loving relationship. American life coach Ron Jenkins' motto reminds us to *love people, not things* because this is what matters in the final analysis.

There are many different kinds of love. Family bonds run the gamut from the filial connections of siblings and parents, to the romantic/sexual attachment of a mate, to the unconditional love for your own children. Then there is compassion, the care and empathy you extend to all beings, the ones you know well, not so well, and even the ones you don't know at all.

For the purpose of this discussion I will focus on unconditional love, which in reality, transcends categorical definition. The more unconditional love we have flowing into and out of our lives, the better for us individually and collectively. However, considering the divorce rate, this kind of love seems to be in short supply among North American men and women.

When money takes precedence, love takes a back seat. The culturally instilled fear of "not having enough" drives us to work harder for money. Pain, and fear of pain, is a very big motivator in our present society. Pain and pleasure can play major roles in the way we balance our life needs. Many of us make decisions on the likelihood of suffering hardship. If we are scared we don't have enough to pay the bills, we may forget obligations to our physical and mental health, and relationships.

*This is not an excuse, folks* – if you have a pair of shoes, a meal a day, and access to public transportation, as do the majority of divorced North Americans, you are rich by world standards, and *your preoccupation with money may be based on perception, not reality.*

A lot of us worry about where we'll end up. But unless you are actually bankrupt, evicted, living on the street, begging for bus fare, and don't know where your next meal is coming from (and some of us are) – you only think you have an excuse.

When fear of material poverty preoccupies us, we end up poor in other ways. Fear is a bigger drain on energy, ambition, enthusiasm, and dreams, than poverty, shame, old age, and sickness combined. But fear is a state of mind that can be overcome. Art from the truly inspired – a writer like Shakespeare, or an artist like Michelangelo – transcends death.

Ideas about pain and pleasure create the mindsets we inhabit. If we focus on pain, as too many of us do, the pain will only expand. The mind is like a highway, that flows from past to distant future.

The problem for many of us is focusing on past pain, and projecting it into the future. This pain can blind attempts to love. Overwhelming pain can kill what love we have.

If we use pain and pleasure to control others – the so-called carrot and stick – we too may come to expect others to goad us into action, and validate our accomplishments. But can we really call them accomplishments, and will they really be ours?

Just as a parent, fearing the hypothetical outcome disobedience might bring, may use threats or rewards to motivate a non-compliant child, an emotionally needy person may try to buy or bully the affection of others. In fact, it's not altogether inconceivable that children who receive a lot of external motivation from their parents grow up into externally motivated adults.

We need to be aware that threats and promises, violence and rewards, are extremes on the same continuum. They don't instil inner discipline, according to parenting expert Barbara Coloroso (1995). When you let them rule, pleasure and pain teach that the outside world is in control. Although they wear different masks, both are responses to external stimuli, and essentially the same thing.

Stimulus-response psychology is the view that the environment controls our behaviour. Ivan Pavlov pioneered this theory when he rang a dinner bell to prompt dogs to salivate. Human beings are vulnerable to the same kind of conditioning, but unlike other animals, have the awareness to consciously change conditioned responses. To bypass the limiting beliefs set by this theory – and still held by many – we must teach self-responsibility and free choice by example. When we know we have choice, we are able to address our perceived or real fear in a proactive manner.

Self-responsibility applies as much to love as it does to discipline. Sadly, however, many of us wait for others to tell us we are good enough to be loved. The inadequacy may be imagined, but the insecurity is real. If we learn to be responsible to ourselves, and love who we are, we can love others without neediness. When we take responsibility for our own thoughts, emotions, and actions, and stop blaming circumstances or people, we transcend joy and pain altogether. As Rudyard Kipling wrote in the poem *If,* oft-quoted in graduation cards:

*"If you can dream – and not make dreams your master,*
*If you can think – and not make thoughts your aim,*
*If you can meet with Triumph and Disaster*
*And treat those two impostors just the same,*

\* \* \*

*If you can fill the unforgiving minute*
*With sixty seconds' worth of distance run,*
*Yours is the earth and everything that's in it,*
*And – which is more – you'll be a Man, my son!"*
[Or an adult, daughter.]

Pain is real, but a large part of the perception of pain – suffering – originates in *fear*. Suffering is self-created. Fear arises from the thoughts we create in our heads.

This isn't new thinking. It also happens to be the central teaching of Siddhartha Gautama Buddha – the Four Noble Truths. (Boorstein, 1998.)

The first of these truths is that life is fundamentally unsatisfying because of its impermanence. Nothing lasts forever.

The second talks about the difference between the inevitable pains of life and the extra pain – suffering – created in the mind that clings to attachments.

The third is the promise that peace of mind and a contented heart are not dependent on external circumstances, and that suffering can be overcome.

The fourth Noble Truth, the Eightfold Path of Practice, follows the promise of peace with instructions on morals and meditation practice.

Perhaps my university psychology professor had the Noble Truths in mind when he told us people create more fear in their heads than they ever experience. When fear rules us, we limit our own potential.

One of the greatest fears in our society is the pain of being alone and unloved. To be loved, we need to first love ourselves. Sparkle Kitty is able to love generously because she loves who she is.

Loving who you are doesn't mean you are self-centred. In fact, you're more likely to be self-absorbed when you are conflicted. Loving who you are is more about being friends with yourself. It's a prerequisite for love and loyalty to others, talents all our greatest human beings have had.

# 1  The Power of Love

Civil rights leader Martin Luther King, Jr. knew that to overcome injustice and inequality people must move beyond their individual needs. This is next to impossible if we aren't happy with ourselves. Toward the end of his life, King knew his activism was putting his life in jeopardy, but he persisted. He was assassinated April 4, 1968, while planning a multiracial march for anti-poverty legislation in Memphis, Tennessee.

It's no coincidence King's story has much in common with Mahatma Gandhi's. Gandhi was King's inspiration.

Mohandas Karamchand Gandhi knew, as did King, just how much love has to do with civility in our world. Called "Mahatma" or "Great Soul" by his followers, Gandhi was both a political and spiritual leader. He used passive resistance, part of his philosophy of "satyagraha" or "truth-force," and "ahimsa" or "non-violence," to eventually lead India to independence from Britain in 1947.

After his professional education in Britain, and early law practice in South Africa, he returned to his native India in 1915 and gave up Western ways – adopting a life of abstinence. He asserted the unity of all people under one God, and preached Christian, Muslim and Hindu ethics. (He did not draw distinctions between the oriental traditions of Hinduism, Buddhism and Jainism.) His civil disobedience campaigns led to his imprisonment on several occasions, but hunger strikes forced his release, thanks to the power of his following. He opposed the Indian caste system, and defended the lowest caste, the "untouchables." His newspaper, *Harijan*, was named for them.

Gandhi was deeply distressed by the religious division of India and Pakistan, and resorted to fasts and prayer vigils when violence broke out. He was fatally shot on one such vigil in 1948, by a Hindu extremist who objected to Gandhi's tolerance for Muslims.

Gandhi is remembered for his pacifism and non-violence, but these were rooted in his belief in love:

"Love is no love which asks for a return."

"The law of love knows no bounds of space or time."

"Love is the subtlest force in the world." (www.mkgandhi.org/)

Gandhi called his peace work an "experiment" on the grandest scale he could make possible. He taught Indians to be non-confrontational with the British, knowing the British could not hurt them without provocation.

King became a disciple of the movement, and years later would write of Gandhi's "ahimsa":

*"The highest expression of non-injury is love and I think many people misunderstand love at this point. They think that when you talk about 'love' you are talking about sentimental, affectionate emotion and I would be the first to say that this is absurd; it is nonsense to urge oppressed people to love their oppressors in an affectionate sense. This is very difficult and almost impossible....*

*"So when I try to explain what I mean by this 'love stuff' I turn to the Greek language. It has a word, agape. Now agape is more than aesthetical or romantic love. Agape is more than a friendship. Agape is understanding, creative, redemptive, good-will for all men. It is an overflowing love which seeks nothing to return. Theologians would say that it is love of God operating in the human heart." (www.mkgandhi.org/)*

One of *my* favourite teachers, William Glasser, taught me many things, the most important being that this kind of love begins with self-acceptance. It is my responsibility and choice to love myself. *Nobody* can find love without taking the action of looking and asking for it. And only I can determine my self-acceptance, no one else.

The process of reaching self-acceptance is congruent with what I call the **Four Phases of Love:**

1. In the first phase, the person is looking at obtaining love. They depend on others like a new-born child does. They need touch, sounds, and attention from the outside to know they are loved.

2. All children at around age two start to develop self-love. This is the beginning of their ego development. They like who they are, and accept themselves. If they do not continue to develop to the next phase they will slip back to Phase 1 as they get older.

3. Unconditional self-love can take place only when you are independent of others' views and opinions of you. You are free and in charge of your ability to love yourself and others.

4. Unconditional relationship and community love happens when you are able to love the members of your family and community independently of their actions or behaviour.

It is important to observe how many adults are still in Phase 1. To have a healthy, independent relationship, both parties need to at least be in Phase 3. It would be interesting to know how many of the partners – among the 50 percent of all couples who get divorced or separated – occupy Phase 1. In their case, even "starting over" accomplishes nothing, if they stay in Phase 1, and never work through self-acceptance.

Material preoccupations, as we've seen, are one reason people forget love. Another reason people forget love is lack of respect. We all need to feel *respected*, for the sake of equality, if nothing else. I believe we need to respect others. For me, respect happens when you:

**R**ealize others have their opinions and views, as do you,

**E**mpathize with others' circumstances,

**S**tandardize attention, treating all people equally,

**P**olitely and civilly interact with others on every level of involvement,

**E**thically and morally deal with others,

**C**ommunicate clearly – being aware of your verbal and non-verbal signals,

**T**olerate others. Everyone is an individual – be patient and non-judgmental

If we believed compassion could accomplish more than aggression, we might not do so much rushing and complaining. Have you ever felt frustrated when stuck in traffic? It's a wonder that road rage isn't more widespread. Would we be in such a hurry if we had more humility?

If we each consider humility as a way of life, and acknowledge others, we can build bridges for love in our society. Charles Schwab, the great steel executive, built his company on the premise of approval and encouragement of people. His success was natural.

He believed that by recognizing the value of individuals, they would be more inclined to help each other. When people work together with love, they feel safe. When they aren't ruled by fear, people feel authentic – that they have a place of importance and value. The same rules apply as much to society as business.

Inside, we all want a more loving society. Why aren't we living it? With all of the negativity in the world, many find it hard to show love. But if we can go to the moon, we can change society. We have made huge technological advances – now we're talking about Mars – and we still haven't solved some of our most basic human problems. Proof? We still suffer from domestic violence within our very walls and borders.

We've made technology the priority and let character-building slip. Stephen Covey's (1990) research points out how this has happened steadily over the last 200 years. From the 19th to the mid-20th century, all the best "success teaching" was in character building. From the 1950s to today the focus has been on technology. Perhaps we are too ready to take off into outer space, while the human race is losing ground.

Consider the increase in the number of people who are on psychotropic drugs. Unfortunately, too many are continuing to use drugs to find love. If we had much more emphasis on promoting love and caring in our society, I think we would have fewer drug concerns.

Where to start is the challenge. Personally, I would like to see the media actively promote good world events 90 percent of the time, and focus on pain the other 10 per cent, instead of the present, opposite, "impact-oriented" approach. It will take time for a media change to be accepted, although in about ten years' time society could be used to it.

It may take a long time to start change of this magnitude, so in the interim we can only start with ourselves. That is all we can do! If we all made this choice at one time to start loving others and ourselves, the world would be a better place. Even if everyone did not start doing this at the same time, this movement would create the wave needed to engulf the ones who were not ready at the beginning.

Love is a verb. It calls us to action, on behalf of every person in the world.

This requires empathy and active listening.

When Sparkle Kitty plays with her friends, she is quick to pick up the rules of the game, and adapt in a non-judgmental way. She immediately sees the value in what the children are playing. She has the desire to fit into the social interaction, so she is willing to seek out their models of the world quickly so she can understand them, and grow with them in their play. She expects to be accepted, and believes that within minutes she will have a new set of friends. I am amazed every time Sherrie and I stop her play – when we need to go home for supper – she acts as if she is saying goodbye to the best friends in the world. Now I understand, because children live in the moment.

Although children on a playground may compete and argue, they have an underlying compassion for each other. What do they do when a child gets hurt playing? What is their focus? They are concerned that the child is okay, so that they can continue with their game.

*Ten Tips to Increase Your Love for Others:*

1. Do not keep score of what you do. Do kind things because you want to, and expect nothing in return. When you do this, great things will happen.
2. Learn to love yourself first, so you know how to love others. Quantum physics is teaching us that our emotions create energy and a vibration that will attract similar waves of energy. This is a good place to start.
3. Believe that the world is a loving place. If we all thought this, what impact would it have? We need to start with our own thoughts. Take responsibility for these first.
4. Stop more now than later to enjoy nature. Become aware how beautiful our planet really is.
5. Make a daily meditation and commitment to loving others unconditionally.
6. Define love with your partner, and be specific so each of you knows you are being loved the way you want to be loved.
7. All human beings are doing the best they can with what they have at any moment in time. We may not agree with or condone their behaviour, but we should accept the fact human beings make mistakes, and learn to forgive and forget. Mistakes are how we learn.
8. Surround yourself with people who want to think the way you do. Don't stay in situations that are painful or hurtful. The first step is to create a supportive environment. We can always choose our environments. We may need to give up something to get what we really want – that is what choice is.
9. Love is a process and not an event. It's a time investment – not a capital investment. You can't just sit back and watch the investment grow. It is important that you act daily to continue banking your love for family and community.
10. Find at least one role model to remind you of the path. There is no question that when we all are able to show love for others, the world will be a better place.

If we could bring the unspoken rules of playground play into our adult world, we'd have a lot less conflict. The world is nothing more than a giant playground for us all. We can love or fight ourselves – and others. The choice is ours, and we need to make it for ourselves.

*In closing . . .*

We cannot change the world alone. We can only control what we do. But once we start, one person will influence another, and create a wave of influence that ultimately spreads worldwide. The world is ripe for the change. People are educated. They know they want more love in the world. Now we are ready to learn how to realize it. Scott Peck (1997), the famous psychiatrist, imparted three powerful ideas on this process; the first being that just because it is simple does not mean it is easy; the second, if we all thought of the world as a pond, our lifelong actions would be consolidated in one pebble; thirdly, we need to have problems so we can grow. If each one of us threw ourselves wholly and without reservation into this new pond – by living life with love – the ripples of each person's loving actions would eventually overlap, and the positive interference would create a great synergistic power.

For more world love we need to start first with ourselves. Children know what we as adults have forgotten. Adults run religions and government. The only way to have *world love* and peace is for the people of the world to change, one by one. The one part of the world you can control is you, and what you do.

Sparkle Kitty Coaching:
Love makes the world go around the right way!

1 THE POWER OF LOVE

## Sparkle Action

The activities listed below will help you study this chapter, and obtain the learning from it. The way to enhance your knowledge is by studying and self-reflection, and then practice.

1. On a scale of 1 (low) and 10 (high), how much are you already living this childmind principle today? _____

2. List three points from this chapter that may have had special significance for you:

   a) _____
   b) _____
   c) _____

3. How will this principle help you in each of the five *life balance* areas?
   In the space provided, be specific about each area:

   Health: _____

   Self: _____

   Relationships: _____

   Career: _____

   Money: _____

4. What is one insight you believe you need to act on?
   _____

   What is your action plan?
   _____

   List the steps here:
   _____
   _____
   _____

# Chapter 2
# The Power of Courage

*"I can DO it!" – Sparkle Kitty*

WHEN Emily goes to the dentist, she needs an antibiotic to protect her heart. A nick in her gum in the dentist's chair carries a risk of endocarditis – a bacterial condition to which her scarred heart lining will always be susceptible.

The antibiotic is usually a pill, but when Emily was two, we took her to Halifax for a medical procedure unrelated to her heart. That time she needed an intravenous antibiotic. You don't want to fool around with endocarditis – it typically involves a three-month hospital stay, and one in four cases is fatal.

The nurses tried and tried to place the intravenous needle into those tiny little arms. But Emily was bruised, bleeding, and completely traumatized before they found a vein. Finally, the doctor came in and asked her how she was now, and through her sobs she managed, "Just great," with a tear-streaked smile. This sums up her fighting spirit.

Any time Sparkle Kitty starts something new, like dance or girl scouts, *I* am the one hoping she will be okay. I wonder, completely unnecessarily, if will she will be intimidated by the new situation. The reality is that I, as a parent, need to have the courage to let her go. She is so brave, she is always ready to just do it.

I am truly amazed by the courage our children have. If you have ever visited a cancer ward for children, you will witness courage that is beyond words. But the courage of children is all around you. When I watch Sparkle Kitty play with her brothers, they are fearless. Nothing stops them from trying new things.

She's not self-conscious. She works away at things even if she looks silly. She gives everything her best effort.

Many adults do not have a child's courage to try new and different things. Adults are more prone to creating excuses and frames of reference that limit their potential. The fact is, many of us adults have a difficult time just starting new things.

Courage is also what helps us make life decisions. Many have difficulties making big and little decisions. Unfortunately, what some of us don't realize is that when we do not choose to address a life challenge – by procrastination or inaction – that is a decision too. Many times we are put in situations we did not create, that require us to make a decision. The choice will ultimately be ours. Whatever decision we make will require us to have the internal strength to follow through. I believe the first step is half the trip. I see too many people get so stuck in their thinking they never do anything. Thinking about what you wished you'd done won't help – especially when you are 90 years old.

Courage can also be described as the will to get through what is in front of us. For many, getting through life is a major challenge. Many people are bored by their day-to-day routines, but stay in situations they do not like because they lack the courage to do something different. Why? The *fear* of not being able to find something better. We all have our own definitions for courage. What is courage for you?

The shackle holding us all back is *fear*. Fear runs rampant in our population. Now, we do need some fear to stay alive. For example, I fear walking in the middle of a highway in the dark. There is something about the thought of a large truck hitting me that stops me from doing this. We really do need some fear to keep us safe and making healthy choices. However, when we go to the extreme of fearing everything, it serves no purpose. It is draining away our ability to live. There are many ways of defining fear. I define it dwelling upon a future that isn't guaranteed, evidence that bad things can happen, or putting off action because of a risk perceived to be too great.

The result is that fear stops forward progress. It paralyzes to an extent determined by the degree of fear – from hang-ups to extreme terror. For example, a phobia is a fear that is stored unconsciously. The fear may not even make sense to you, but you may still have a hard time working through it. It can be very difficult to conquer a true phobia by pushing yourself – your legs may literally give out.

Courage is more than human will. Will is taking action despite the fear. But will alone may not solve recurring phobias, panic attacks, post traumatic stress disorder, or other disorders which originate in fear. There is a lot of help available now, and *you do not need to live with these highly treatable conditions.*

(Please note: If you are one of these people, your doctor can refer you to a specialist who helps people overcome phobias. There are strategies that will help.)

Human will is about the drive and determination to get the life you want, and being persistent in working toward it. Courage develops with the persistent application of human will. Experience shows us our talents and limits. A glimpse of our potential gives us the courage to continue. Courage builds momentum. The first step is to make your decision to change.

We are all faced with our own mortality. We know we are going to die. I find it interesting most of us accept this fact, and do not dwell on it daily. However, many of us are so easily stuck in life's little concerns. Richard Carlson (1998) talks about letting go of the little things that can rule us. Among suggested tips: "Will it matter a year from now? Drop the stuff that won't."

I have a theory called the 98-2 theory. It goes like this: if 98 percent of life is fine, and 2 percent is troubling, if we continue to focus on the 2 percent it will become the 98 percent, and eventually overwhelm us.

Beware of the small things that can turn into big things if they aren't addressed. Usually all that is required is communication. But for many people, effective communication is a major hurdle, a hurdle they may need courage to clear.

Take a rude boss, for example. Faced with one, many of us do nothing. Why? Because we lack the courage to trust that we have the skills to address this kind of inappropriate behaviour. Too many accept for a long time the pain that a rude boss can project. In many cases, incidents with superiors create the stage where most of the actual intimidation is really only happening in our heads.

Regardless if the fear is real or perceived, people will go to great lengths to avoid confronting it. The first step to deal with situations like the rude boss is to deal with ourselves, and learn to challenge our own thinking. Acknowledge that many create beliefs that lead us to labelling people, places, and things. For example, what if the boss was not rude, and was only doing their job? How does it help us to challenge and stop labelling others?

Without courage, we aren't free. As the Spanish saying goes, "A vivir como miedo es como a vivir medias," – a life lived in fear is a life half-lived.

We are all offered the freedom of choice. We need freedom. According to William Glasser, it is a genetic need, and an internal drive. Without courage – not to mention some education, and some money – freedom can appear difficult to achieve.

Life is a journey involving constant decision-making. According to renowned psychiatrist Viktor Frankl, you have the right to make your own choices regardless of the situation. Joel Barker (1992), the popular teacher of paradigms – views of the world – wrote a great deal on the effect of our paradigms on our behaviour, and how these have a direct impact on the way we respond and behave daily at work and home. Is the cup half-full or half-empty? Most of us have heard this expression before. The truth is, it is both. The way you see it depends on your model of the world.

Many people do not live life. If and when they can turn things around, they create a whole new paradigm of living. When we learn we are not victims of the world and can take action to obtain what we want, we are free. Courage is an important principle in decision-making, not only in taking the plunge, but following through:

**Sparkle Kitty's Decision Model**

- Determine your options – researching all that is possible.
- Evaluate the pros and cons of each.
- Choose the top three.
- Invite input from a trusted friend and/or associate.
- Stick with your gut instincts – they are usually right.
- Initiate your plan.
- Observe what is happening, and be prepared to make adjustments.
- Never give up – don't be discouraged if you need to make a new plan.

You will always be faced with the need to make decisions. Every decision you make sets the scene for another. If you don't get what you want, you now have the decision of what you will do next. The process of making decisions is life-long, and one faced by every living form on this planet.

**Ten Tips to Develop Courage**

1. Adopt a good decision-making strategy (e.g., Sparkle Kitty's Decision Model).

2. Start using it – it may take more time and practice than you think to master this important skill, so be patient.

3. Look beyond the situation facing you.
   (a) Imagine it five years after a successful outcome.
   (b) Return to the now – are you still afraid?
   (c) Look through the event and see no fear.
   (d) Repeat steps a through c until the fear diminishes.

4. Courage is well-thought thoughts, not crazy and overwhelming emotion. I promote courage, not craziness. Be smart!

5. Be clear on your outcome. Know exactly what you want before you take any action. This will help you avoid being ruled by emotion.

6. Always take ownership of your actions, no excuses. Never blame others for your actions. What you do you must accept. This is courage.

7. Practice talking to yourself about what you can do and how you can be successful. Practice building your courage by ensuring you use positive thinking.

8. Have a support group of strong relationships in your life. If you don't have one, get busy!

9. Write out what you want, and read it aloud before you take action. This will help you clarify your intentions. It is also a good practice run.

10. Be sure that your courage is never at the expense of another person in a mean or angry way. Then take action! May the force be with you!
    We all have different levels of courage. Take a moment and explore yours:
    (a) If you had more courage, how would this help you in your life?
    (b) Do you see courage as an issue that you struggle with?
    (c) Why do you avoid things that bother you?
    (d) What is one thing you could do today to start to develop your courage?

Often we think of people who have courage as falling into two categories – leaders and aggressors. Don't be misled. Courage is not aggression. School yard bullies are aggressive because they need the security of picking on those they perceive to be weaker. Often the motivation is, better to be the perpetrator than the victim. However, there is a line between assertiveness and aggression. With courage, we rarely need to be aggressive (only when called upon to protect ourselves or others). In this age of the world, having courage means being able to act on a life challenge, and follow through. Our physical survival and "fight or flight response" is rarely the issue it was for past generations.

And yet, many of our children feel unsafe on a daily basis, and as high school shootings attest, some of them *are* unsafe. When I watch Sparkle Kitty on a playground, I see evidence that she only believes all the children on the playground want to be her friends. She truly believes they will accept her. She expects people to like her. She does so because she first of all believes that she is a good person. She likes and accepts others because she is able to do this for herself. She never thinks of judging people – she is just interested in getting to know them.

She had taken her hair out of braids before school one morning recently, and a classmate teased her about her fuzzy hair. When she recounted the experience at home later that day, she said, "First I was upset, and then I said to him, 'I'm sorry you don't like it, because *I* do'."

She's a little more sophisticated now, at the age of seven. But I remember another incident when she was only four. She was playing in the yard at pre-school with a little boy who ordinarily was very well behaved. He decided that day that he was a dinosaur, and he was going to eat her. He closed his hands around her throat and started to choke her.

When Sherrie picked her up that day, the pre-school staff briefed her on the incident.

"So what did you do?" Sherrie asked her.

"Well, Mummy, I bit him," she answered. "He scared me, Mummy, I was having trouble breathing. I bit him really hard, and then I kicked him, and ran away, and told him not to touch me ever again."

There are situations where it is important to speak your mind, and draw the line. And Sparkle Kitty's instincts, as far as Sherrie and I have been able to tell, are pretty reliable.

When we lived in North Carolina for a year, Emily was attracted to children of diverse racial backgrounds. For a while, she wanted to be black. She thought black skin was beautiful, and wanted to be better accepted by her black friends. She was a little worried about this. Then she considered the fact that she was not black, that she was Emily Howatt, and she was okay the way she was.

For Emily to be happy, she needed to start with self-acceptance: "I am okay as a person." When we start out this way, we are on the road to self-love. She figured out that as a white child, she could and did have the knowledge and skills to be accepted by her black friends and others.

Wouldn't you like to live in a world where people did not judge each other? One of the most painful experiences of being human is feeling we won't be good enough or won't be accepted by others. Ahead of bullying, fear of rejection is what preoccupies the majority of schoolchildren – not their marks.

How many adults do you know who really like themselves? Do you like who you are? Too many of us judge ourselves unfairly, without evidence. One of the biggest challenges in our society is healthy self-esteem. Many people question their self-worth on a daily basis. Too many of us see ourselves how we imagine others see us. Too often pain is the biggest roadblock to our taking chances. The pain we know is better than the pain of trying – or failure! Too many people learn to live life settling for second best. They know they are not happy, but brainwash themselves into thinking things are okay. Their present pain is paradoxically the main motivator to stay passive; the result – they couldn't be further from the life they want. How many doors do we close before even trying to open them? The key to them all is our self-esteem – the will to believe in ourselves!

When I asked my general practitioner about the majority of his patient base, he told me that a lot of his patients have talked themselves into being sick and stressed. Is it possible that some diseases originate with low self-esteem? Many people cannot accept that their own mind state plays a role in their illness. When people are not happy with themselves they are at greater risk of becoming sick. This illness could run a continuum from a minor cold to major cancer. There is more science now that ascribes a greater role to psychosomatic illness (created from inside our minds). When people do not like who they are, they are really at the mercy of what others tell them they are worth. Do you know these people? Can you relate to this?

Albert Bandura (1997), the famous researcher of human behaviour, wrote a great deal on the topic of self-development. A brief overview of his main teaching shows how he breaks down the steps needed for positive self-esteem. The basic foundation of self-esteem is to like who we are. To do this, we need to know we are okay, and believe in ourselves. The steps to a positive self-esteem are:

1. *Self-Efficacy* – one's impression of what one is capable of doing.
2. *Self-Competency* – the ability to put those skills to use.
3. *Self-Esteem* – the attitude we have about ourselves in the moment.

These three things are the foundation of our self-concept (ego.) Although the word "ego" has a negative connotation for some, a certain amount of it is healthy. You can determine a person's ego strength by their self-esteem; the greater the self-esteem, the greater the ego strength.

When I observe Sparkle Kitty engaging new friends on a playground, I see she has knowledge, ability and attitude in place together *like a rock*. When she is on the playground she is like a magnet – children will come to her. Although if you watch, you will see this happens to other children all the time as well.

Let's look at the adult world. Think about a party you have attended lately. Where do most people gravitate? They usually surround the person who is the life of the party. Why do they do this? People like being around those who are fun, positive, and bring joy to others. It's true that outgoing people may sometimes be faking it, but when we present confidence, we will be treated as if we have it.

The fact is when we lack self-confidence we are at the mercy of what others give us. Self-esteem starts with how see ourselves. There is no greater predictor of our future success and happiness.

Glasser has hit on a nugget of truth, teaching what he calls Internal Locus of Control, another way of approaching self-responsibility. You may already be familiar with this idea if you have ever read the work of existentialist philosophers. This is the idea that all behaviour is internally motivated, and we always have choice as to how we are going to respond to the outside world. Here are the tenets of Glasser's Choice Theory:

1. We all perceive the world through five senses.

2. We have a database of everything we know, and are always comparing information that comes in with what we know.

3. We all have pictures in our head of what we want (e.g., for love, I see my wife, Sherrie).

4. All our wants come from five basic genetic needs – love, recognition and self-power, fun, freedom, and survival.

5. All of the five basic genetic needs are programmed in our heads, and we are driven internally to satisfy them.

6. All of our behaviour is our best attempt to meet one or more of the above needs.

7. All our behaviours are learned, so we can only do what we know or what we create.

8. We are always evaluating information that we take in through our five senses, comparing what we have against what we want.

9. When there is a difference between what we have and want, we have no choice except to behave.

10. All behaviour is total. Our actions, thoughts, feeling, and physiology are connected. We have 100 percent control of our actions, partial control of our thoughts and feelings, and our physiology has no choice except to follow our thoughts and actions.

11. To take charge of oneself, one always has choice over how to act.

12. Nothing in the past can make you do anything in the present.

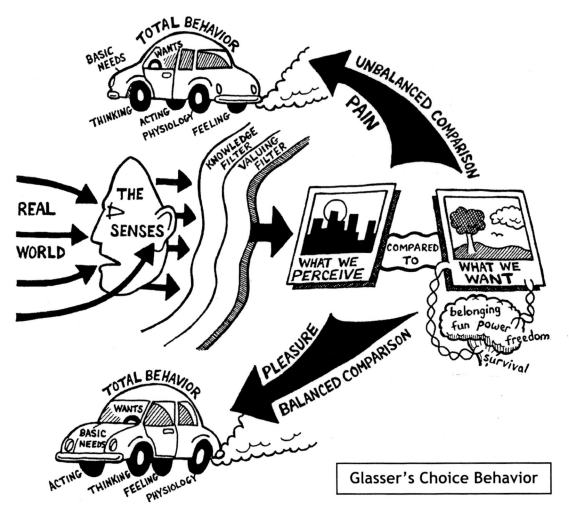

Glasser's Choice Behavior

In the above graphic you will see how we take information in from the outside world. Once we take it in through the five senses we are comparing it to our "album" of quality pictures that we choose to represent our basic needs. No two people will have the exact same pictures in their head. Whenever there is a difference between what we have and what we want, we become frustrated. We will continue to feel frustrated until we meet our needs. This is why some people will stay depressed or anxious for long periods of time. Until their needs are met, they will feel unbalanced.

This is also why some people will choose addictions to satisfy an unmet need like self-worth. People can have many different unmet needs going on at one time. Your brain has the ability to continue to function even when your needs aren't being met.

When we have more self-confidence, we have more of what is called threshold tolerance for unmet needs (although when confident, we're more capable of having our needs met). When we are able to be more patient, we can delay gratification and expectations for relief. This is useful, because life is a process, and we cannot always have what we want, when we want it. However, if we have confidence, and take the right action, we have, with time, a greater chance of getting what we want in life.

When we are able to operate from an internal locus of control, as Glasser refers to it – "authentically," as Jean-Paul Sartre termed it; "authentically empowered," as talk-show hostess Oprah Winfrey is fond of saying; "self-referred," as Deepak Chopra says; or "independent of the good opinion of others"; as Wayne Dyer calls it – we will no longer be the victims of others' perceptions. We will always know we have a choice. As all of these freedom fighters would tell you, not taking action to improve your life is also a choice.

Internal control is a new doctrine for many. However, those of us who practice it daily are much happier than we were. The great thing is that all children start out believing they have the choice to do what they want. We as adults condition them to the point where they disbelieve, and we end up suppressing their ability to make decisions. (For more information, visit Glasser's website at www.glasserinst.com.)

*In closing . . .*

Developing the principle of courage will open your heart, mind, and soul to every other childmind principle. It's easy to confuse the memory of childhood fears with the notion that childhood is fearful – so many fears to be overcome. But as adults we may carry around as significant a "load" of hang-ups. We may have different fears, not fewer ones; for in truth, the only fears we human beings are born with are of falling and loud noises. Every other fear is learned. The natural state of childmind is a fearless one. Where our adult fears are concerned, it may take time, practice, and possibly coaching (which is fine) to conquer them. Whether we need help is not the point – but whether we act.

> Sparkle Kitty Coaching:
>
> I know I can if I say so.

## Sparkle Action

The activities listed below will help you study this chapter, and obtain the learning from it. The way to enhance your knowledge is by studying and self-reflection, and then practice.

1. On a scale of 1 (low) and 10 (high), how much are you already living this childmind principle today? _____

2. List three points from this chapter that may have had special significance for you:

   a) _____

   b) _____

   c) _____

3. How will this principle help you in each of the five *life balance* areas?
   In the space provided, be specific about each area:

   Health: _____

   Self: _____

   Relationships: _____

   Career: _____

   Money: _____

4. What is one insight you believe you need to act on?
   _____

   What is your action plan?
   _____

   List the steps here:
   _____
   _____
   _____

# Chapter 3
# The Power of Fun

*"It's your turn to play with me!"* – *Sparkle Kitty*

THE next most important thing for Sparkle Kitty besides air is fun. This is a conclusion I have reached watching her, but I believe it's true of all children. I also believe this remains true as we get older, too – we all want to have fun. Do you like to have fun? Most of us would like to answer, "Yes!" Sadly, many of us also have to add the "but" part! This seems to mean we want fun, but don't believe we have enough time or money. Many of us make rules that prevent us from having fun.

Sparkle Kitty is positively addicted to having fun. When she is not having fun, she often shuts down. She says she is bored: "What's the point when you can't have fun?" Is this true for adults, as well? What do we do when we lack fun or passion in our lives?

When I say fun I am not talking about the artificial funs that are obtained at the local pub. I am talking about the fun of getting up and being truly excited about what the day will bring, being excited about discovering the joy in each day, wherever we are – work, school or home.

If you recall, Tom Hanks' character in the movie Forrest Gump was extremely childlike, but in a way that served not only his own survival, but that of the others around him. He risked his own life without question to save his battalion in the Vietnam War, was wounded and later decorated – although he appeared "simple" to many of the people around him. Simplicity, however, is a hallmark of childmind.

Gump's famous line was, "Life is like a box of chocolates, you never know what you're gonna get." The metaphor begins with the very pleasurable theme of chocolate. How may people find joy in chocolate? If life is what we want it to be, can we afford *not* to have fun? I think not – fun is a necessary and major driving life principle.

Are you a person who has a great deal of fun daily?

Almost every day, when she comes home from school, Sparkle Kitty goes down to her tickle trunk to dress up. Sherrie has stocked this trunk with second-hand clothing, and vacation finds, including a Mexican sombrero.

Sparkle Kitty gets out of her school clothes as quickly as she can, to put on something interesting. And what does she do? A free spirit, she loves to dance. Sherrie chose not to put her in ballet classes, unwilling to rob her of the natural freedom of movement she displays while dancing, although Sparkle Kitty did take a theatre class, where she could revel in the opportunity to express herself without restriction.

She loves to play on her own, too, and will set up elaborate tea parties for her stuffed animals and Barbie dolls. She lines them up on the bed. They've all got distinctly different personalities and voices.

She also loves to make tea for Sherrie. And although circuses, beaches, and family vacations have all been thrilling for her, she is quite content to make up her own games. The ability to play is something that some of us lose as we age. But we all seem to start out with it. Have you ever watched a child who was in a safe and loving environment not play? I have not.

I believe that play and the need for fun is an internal *need* we all have. It may not be as obvious as money, career, relationships, self-worth, and health, but it is just as important. According to Glasser, fun is a genetic need we are all driven to meet. We have no choice but to be motivated for fun, some more than others. Whatever the level of fun for a person, we all need it in our lives. It is where we derive our passion and enjoyment of life, our "joie de vivre." Fun is a feeling that helps people determine if life is enjoyable or not, and therefore key to sanity.

What is the relationship between fun and self-acceptance?

Would you say people who like themselves have more fun than people who do not? I think they do.

In my past, I worked a great deal with addictions. Today, approximately 32 percent of the total North American population has some kind of addiction. Most addictions arise from the person's need for more fun and pleasure, or as an escape from the pressures of daily life. We all associate fun with pleasure, which is a key element for reducing life stress, and relief from perceived pain. When we have fun, we release chemicals in our brains that relieve worry, and fill us with a sense of well-being. People who do not feel or recognize this sense of well-being will become satisfied with artificial states as a substitute. When a person continues this cycle, they can become addicted. Over time, most people using chemicals to excess will eventually become driven both physically and psychologically to obtain the drug (e.g., alcohol). We call this chemical dependency.

Children are mostly all positively addicted to play, and are driven to have fun. They do not see the need for drugs. Why? They don't know these shortcuts exist. They know that if they want to have fun they have to take action. What is the lesson here? What would our lives be like if we were all able to create fun like a child?

What concerns me is that there seems to be a great sense of impending *doom* in our society. Too many people feel that they and the world are hopeless, and they project these feelings onto others. And yet, Mother Teresa walked the streets of Calcutta with a sense of hope. Surrounded by tragedy, her will and thinking alone reduced pain for millions. How could one person do this? She could because of the joy and pleasure she got from helping others.

Would you have more safe and healthy fun if you could? Of course. However, many of us have forgotten how to have fun. We get caught up worrying too much about "making it," and forget to live it! Let's start with where you are, and move to incorporate more fun. And fun involves a certain amount of freedom.

Enjoyment that doesn't come at the expense of others is key here. I find that I do my best learning when I am having fun. How about you? Do you learn more when you are having fun? Do you remember more of what has happened when you are having fun?

The emotional reason we all can remember the fun times is biochemical. We all have the learning drugs involved for memory, one of the most prominent being norepinephrine. When we are having a good time, this drug is in abundance. This is one of the primary drugs responsible for assisting us to store fun times in memory. It stores all the details of what we were doing and who we were with when we had this fun. This will create a file that we will anchor in our body as a fun file. That is why we do not forget what we enjoy doing.

The challenge for humans is that addictions and events we enjoy do the same thing to the brain. In the case of addictions, no matter which drug – alcohol, caffeine or tobacco – the chemicals get us high. The brain stores this addictive behaviour as an attempt to get fun. Most addicts never forget their choice of drug. Although they know the drug is bad for them, they have somehow fixed in their brain the idea that it will truly create less pain and more pleasure. This is why addictions are so tough to overcome.

Sometimes a child will identify one parent as being more fun than the other. The main reason for this is that this parent usually has spent more time in play activities. To store an event as fun, we need to perceive we have had fun. We are the judges of what is fun for us, and what isn't. In my mind, it is important to say that all fun that is true fun only uses the natural chemicals the body makes, and none from the outside. All outside chemicals that are used to create fun are what I call artificial fun enhancers. They only provide a temporary sense of well-being.

To have fun is a challenge if you do not know how to have healthy and safe fun. We make schedules of the things we may not like to do, like changing the oil in our cars, paying our bills, grocery shopping, and visiting the dentist. But how many of us consciously schedule fun into our days? Yes, many of us get it somehow and some way, but few of us plan it. When I think about all the animals in this world, we are the only ones who can really plan out elaborate fun. We make theme parks, multiplex movie theatres, ice rinks, casinos, and concert stages – all for the sole purpose of entertainment. Consider pro sports alone – we will pay a baseball pitcher $15 million for one season, pitching 25 games, in which he may actually pitch only 150 innings. Think about it – this pitcher is making around $100,000 per inning! What price will we pay for fun? *Anything!* The proof is all around us.

What do children need to create fun? Besides their imaginations, not much – a set of pots and pans, maybe. Children have the gift of entertaining themselves. Many of us are so busy we want others to entertain us. Often we do not contribute anything toward entertaining ourselves, except showing up! Take a television and a couch, and you have the makings of a Grade A couch potato! Some of us are so in love with convenience that we have even passed the responsibility of creating our own fun to other people. This isn't so for all of us, but many – especially the 32 percent who have addictions. We can become addicted to letting others entertain us. Look at pro sports again and the money people spend on season tickets and sports paraphernalia. Then look at all the money spent on fitness equipment *that never gets used.*

I think one way to insure you have fun is to engage in a form of recreation that you enjoy. How do you define recreation? Activities such as biking, mountaineering, rock-climbing, skiing, gardening, and martial arts are just a few examples. I believe our minds and bodies benefit a great deal by having the habit of recreation in our lives. I think of recreation as:

**R**elaxing

**E**njoyable

**C**ommitment that you *like* keeping

**R**eleases stress for you

**E**ducational – you get to think and learn as you do

**A**ction-oriented – gets you on the move

**T**ime-balanced, and does not disturb your home life and career

**I**nteresting to you

**O**ngoing, year-round

**N**ever intentionally hurtful to you or others.

The important variable is that you want to do it, and stay committed to it. If you don't enjoy it, and don't get anything out of it, get a new recreational activity!

I hear the excuse of "not having enough time" a great deal. Many people think that they need to manage their time better. Instead, we need to manage our *state* better. At any given time, we are operating in one of the five following states:

1. **Peak Performance State** – we are able to do things easily when we are in our "zone."
2. **Crisis State** – we are doing things urgently (often at the last minute), and never catching up.
3. **Unbalanced State** – we are so stressed that our self-esteem starts to flag, and we don't feel good about ourselves or what we are doing. So instead of tackling the stress, we do something that we think will help us feel better; we have a smoke, a coffee, a drink, or use drugs. A great deal of time is lost in this state.
4. **Trivial State** – we are mentally tired so we do little things to organize and look busy. We look busy, but nothing is getting done. It's like "organizing to organize." Procrastination and perfectionism fall into this category.

5. **Numb State** – we are so fatigued mentally that we tune out the world, and vegetate. Many do this in front of a television, or stare off into space for extended periods of time. We do this to dissociate from the world, so we get a break and stop thinking. But we do it mindlessly, so it doesn't count as meditation, nor is it as productive as reflective thought. No resolutions are made or solutions found.

When life stress hits, many of us believe we can't take care of ourselves in a healthy way, because we have not attached pleasure to exercise. Many people in the early stages of an exercise program fall into the habit of associating their new routine with pain. They create this negative association by reducing the routine to a series of unappealing and uncomfortable steps, through an internal dialogue, such as: "I have to get in my car, drive through traffic, go into a strange locker room, get changed, work out, get all sweaty, shower, get changed again, and drive all the way home." When stress hits, do you want to endure more discomfort or go for the quick fix?

The usual result is that the person stops going to the gym. The negative video we run in our heads stops us before we can create a new one that focuses on the benefits of exercise. In the process of developing healthy habits, many of us are not aware or don't acknowledge our minor successes. We too often forget to use what we learned in Grade 4 and 5 math: fractions and percentages. If I go to the gym, and follow my plan for 30 days, and then on the thirty-first day hit a bunch of life stress, and do not get to the gym for the next three days, does that mean I am a hopeless failure? No! Heck, 30 out of 33 is still 91 percent. That's more than pretty good! In school, that's an 'A' grade. If we can keep an 'A' grade in life, that's *terrific*. But what do most people do? They feel they have slipped and forever lost their momentum, so they quit.

We all make mistakes, but nowhere does it say we need to be perfect. All human beings are fallible, but only when we choose do minor slips become major ones. This is why I ask all my coaching clients to keep a daily journal, so that they can sort fact from opinion, *and keep them separate.* The fact remains, 91 percent is *just great.*

Fun creates the opportunity for the healing drug that we all crave and need. Fun will heal not only the mind, but the body as well. Norman Cousins (1991) healed his own terminal illness by scheduling fun daily. He enjoyed old videos of the Three Stooges every day for thirty minutes. The entertaining television personality Bob

Newhart understands the power of fun, too. He has promoted "fun carts" in hospitals to get as many people laughing as he can. The carts are stocked with a TV, VCR, balloons, and other fun things to play with that help bring joy to people who are sick.

**Ten Tips to Add Fun and Recreation**

1. Make fun important. Even if you have to use your day planner, schedule 15 minutes each day for fun and/or recreation.

2. To have fun, you need to define what healthy fun is for you. Once you do, start to learn how to add it to your life. Be clear on what it is – that is why it is important to write it out. Answer two questions: 1) what is important to you about having fun? 2) What has to happen so you know you are having fun?

3. Start a new and exciting hobby or join a local recreation league.

4. Schedule a vacation that does not make you poor. The planning and the trip can both be fun.

5. If you use chemicals for fun, learn how to live without them. If you can't do this by yourself, get help. Not until you are able to overcome your addictions will you be able to live life to the fullest.

6. Have patience in learning to have fun – it takes time when you have forgotten how.

7. Take a humour workshop – they are great! Practice makes perfect, so practice having fun!

8. Make fun important! If you are going through the motions, the passion isn't there. Attach the passion, and see the fun value skyrocket.

9. Remember the key to fun is self-permission – please give it!

10. Fun is a need, so it will always be there inside you, asking to be fulfilled. To answer the need, you must become aware of the places in your life where you can have more fun and "let the kid out."

*In closing . . .*

We all will be happier and healthier people when we ensure we have lots of healthy and safe fun in our lives. Having fun is part of the reason we are here, and it doesn't have to cost thousands of dollars. Fun is a choice and an attitude. Children can turn a ball and a field into an adventure. Do not limit yourself by rules. Learn to let go and let live. I have heard it said it takes only 13 muscles to smile, and 50 to frown. Smiling creates fewer wrinkles, too. So save some energy and smile, so you have more energy for fun in your life.

> Sparkle Kitty Coaching:
> What would we have if there was no fun? Everybody needs fun!

3   THE POWER OF FUN

## Sparkle Action

The activities listed below will help you study this chapter, and obtain the learning from it. The way to enhance your knowledge is by studying and self-reflection, and then practice.

1. On a scale of 1 (low) and 10 (high), how much are you already living this childmind principle today? _____

2. List three points from this chapter that may have had special significance for you:

   a) _____

   b) _____

   c) _____

3. How will this principle help you in each of the five *life balance* areas?
   In the space provided, be specific about each area:

   Health: _____

   Self: _____

   Relationships: _____

   Career: _____

   Money: _____

4. What is one insight you believe you need to act on?

   _____

   What is your action plan?

   _____

   List the steps here:

   _____

   _____

   _____

Section 2: The Power of Open Mind

# Chapter 4

# The Power of Hope

*"Oh, they're just going to love me!" – Sparkle Kitty*

ON the way to her first day of pre-school in Kentville, when she was three, Sparkle Kitty was a bubbling geyser of excitement. She sat in the back of the van, asking Sherrie question after question about what the kids would be like, what they would be doing, and eating. And finally, she just bubbled over completely, and exclaimed, "Oh, they're just going to love me!"

I hope she can hang on to such vibrant confidence – and I believe she will, if she can keep her knack for positivism.

After her first day of elementary school, in Chapel Hill, North Carolina, when she was reunited with Sherrie, the two were swapping their impressions of the day. Sherrie told her she'd been happy, proud of her, and sad, all at the same time.

"Did you cry?" asked Emily.

"Yes," said Sherrie.

"You were *that* sad?" asked Emily.

"No, I was happy inside," said Sherrie.

"Oh! You had rainbows in your eyes, then. When you're crying, but you're really happy inside, you get rainbows in your eyes," Emily concluded.

A typical morning in my home involves Emily, in pyjamas, with matted hair stuck up in back, bounding into our room for the wake-up call: "Mummy, mummy, mummy! Wake up! It's going to be another great day! You don't want to miss it!"

Mummy comes on!

Mummy never used to be a morning person, but the positivism is contagious.

"Mummy, mummy! The sky is pink! You should see it!"

Mummy could say she was busy, and go load up the wood stove. But she doesn't.

Mummy could get angry when Emily decides to feed the cats early, mixing up their food with milk, and offering them quite a messy feast. But she doesn't.

The positivism is *that* contagious, which is what this chapter is about.

**The Power of Positive Thinking**

Early on, Sparkle Kitty reminded me of what I had forgotten! When we have positive thoughts, we are more able to enjoy the simple moments in life. I was missing them because I was not keeping positive thoughts in my head the majority of the time. Positive thought will crowd out negative, self-defeating thought. When we are positive, we don't have the time or space to be negative. When we were children we did this automatically – unless we were abused in some way.

Psychiatrist David Hawkins (1995) supports positive thinking in his book *Power Vs. Force*. Positive thoughts are positive choice. Hawkins defines force as the impact of our thoughts on our own lives and those of the people around us. In 1975, he began research on the physical response to truth and falsehood, and intimated the existence of a "communal consciousness" or spiritus mundi, which bore similarities to Carl Jung's theories about the unconscious mind.

Jung, a famous student of Freud, taught the world that there is a collective unconscious – a source of wisdom and energy from which all can draw. It's a theory that has gained more supporters than detractors in intervening years, and has provided a stepping stone for other thinkers, like physicist Gary Zukav, who wrote in *The Seat of the Soul* (1990): "The soul of the human species is sometimes called the collective unconscious, but it is not that. It is the soul of humankind. Your soul is a miniature of the soul of the human species. It is a micro of a macro."

Hawkins believes we all will benefit if we put positive thought into this collective pool. His concern is that there are more negatives than positives presently entering this pool. You need only to watch the news on any given night for proof! I believe that children are even more closely connected to the pool of unconscious thought than adults are. Children know the power of creating positive thoughts, and in an undisturbed state, will naturally think them.

*They only stop creating them, I believe, when they are exposed to negativity from the adult world.*

Children are living examples of *positive thought*.

I have one keynote address called, "In life there are no road blocks, we need only accept the detours." In this speech I discuss what I call the four common life challenges that affect the way many of us view the world:

1. Not being good enough
2. Not being smart enough
3. Finding meaning in life
4. Overcoming our limitations

These have been challenges for me in my own life. I have re-examined these problem areas with the insight I gained from Sparkle Kitty. We always have choice to make things great once we accept who and what we are. The road map for all life detours is self-acceptance. If we accept ourselves first, we are well on our way to finding a new beginning. The key is to allow ourselves to have positive thoughts so that we can see the possibilities and opportunities available to us. We must be willing to accept the life lessons when they are presented to us or we will stay where we are.

Sparkle Kitty has taught me that a positive mental attitude for life is a readily available state of mind. We *always* have the option to choose our focus. We can focus on the positive or negative; it is up to us. One day as I was sitting in my living room playing with one of my other children, Thomas, who is two years old, Sparkle Kitty came into the room with tear-filled eyes:

"Jason can't come over to play."

"Is there anything I can do to help?"

"Play with me *now*."

"Sure, what would you like to play?"

"Anything, as long as we are doing it *now*."

Once the three of us started to play, she was completely content. After a short while, I asked her how she was. She replied, "Just great!"

Being a curious student of Sparkle Kitty's, I wanted to know how she was able to go from being sad to happy so quickly. To see what she would say, I offered, "I think it's okay to be sad when people don't want to be with us." She said, "I know, Daddy, but Daddy, I want to only be sad for a second and then I want to be happy. I want to think good things, not bad ones – they're no fun!"

I'm certain she could have turned things around without us, for she already understands that to change a thought, we must change our actions. If Thomas and I hadn't been there with her, she would have quickly become involved in self-play, to attain a happier state of mind. Sparkle Kitty showed me that it is not circumstances that determine our happiness, but the action we take in response to them.

Transforming Negative Thinking

It rarely works when we only say to ourselves that we want to stop negative thinking. Even with our best intentions, it is a challenge to say we will think positively 100 percent of the time. It takes time to reprogram the mind. However, what we can control 100 percent of the time is our actions. In *Choice Theory*, William Glasser argues that our thinking and actions pace our behaviour system. Our feelings and physiology follow the lead of our actions and thinking.

Close your eyes. Feel happy. How did you get happy? You had to have a positive thought attached to an idea or image you associate with being happy. Often what influences a person's mind-state is how they perceive they are motivated – how much control they feel they exert over their own actions, in relation to what is happening around them. For example, many people believe they are motivated by external circumstances. Glasser refers to this as an external locus of control. If someone tells them they are good, they have positive thoughts, and feel good. If someone says that they are not good, they will have negative thoughts, and feel lousy.

In the same way that your focus is your reality, your frame of reference will define what you think. Someone with an external locus of control is often paralyzed simply by what others say. Once they are able to learn to operate from an internal locus of control they truly have the choice of how to respond to the world. The truth is that we can always influence our thinking by the *actions* we take.

How easily are you letting go of your negative thinking? If a five-year-old can ingrain the habit of positive thinking, you don't need a college degree to do it. For Sparkle Kitty, negative thoughts are like dirty little birds landing on her head. She shoos them away as quickly as she can. Now you don't have to get obsessive about this.

Be patient with yourself. When you try too hard *not* to think about something, it can actually be counterproductive. So fill the gap with positive thoughts – it's one way to deal with negative thoughts, and we all need a strategy, or a starting place.

Positive thinking doesn't mean ignoring the facts. To support positive thinking, you have to have positive intentions, or you're just fooling yourself. The person in the mirror is the person who will judge you in the end. The power of positive thinking will lead you through life in a manner that is beneficial not only for you, but others as well.

Norman Vincent Peale sold over 5 million copies of *The Power of Positive Thinking*. This is evidence that many people are striving to think and live positively. Our thoughts, he argues, are a core instrument in a happy, satisfying, and worthwhile life. When we free our mind of the worries that we create by negative thinking, we free up the energy for the lives we *really* want. One research poll I read stated that 60 percent of all people in American society have been a victim of crime; that one in seven carries a gun; and 72 percent of the population is concerned about the environment. This tells me that there are too many people living in fear, accepting negativity as a way of life. It does not have to be this way.

**The Power of Language**

Have you ever noticed the power of language? Think about what happens when someone asks you how you are, and you say "all right" or "okay." Say these words aloud and listen. Feel their impact on your body's physiology. Do they pick up your energy? Do you stay in a flat state? Does this influence your thinking? Taking the action of using positive and powerful language like Sparkle Kitty's "Just great!" line will help you set the tone.

Our assessment of our present sense of wellness will influence our thinking patterns. People will think differently in different states. For example, if you are in a flat state, and someone asks, "How are you?" and you reply, "Fine," you will most likely continue to be in a flat state. A flat state does not mean you are thinking negatively. However, when we are flat we are more likely to fall into negativity. In a flat state, you are more susceptible to influence.

Now if you talk like Sparkle Kitty does, and make a powerful affirmation of well-being, like "Just great!" you are creating strong, healthy vibrations. Words will change your physiology. The Bible says bread will feed our bodies, but words will feed our souls. Beware of the language you use inside your head and outside, in your speech. Are you aware of the words you say? What does that mean to you and your mind? Say "Just great!" aloud with passion a few times. Now observe your body. What is happening? Do you feel more energy? How are you thinking now?

The words we use create our state. Powerful assertions like "Just great!" are emotional drivers, which are the associations we attach to the words we store, so when we say certain words we release these emotional drivers. We do this with both positive and negative words, which conjure up the attached emotions. We anchor emotion to certain words and phrases as we grow older. If you want to expand your positive thinking, become aware of your language. Positive and resourceful language will drive your mind and soul into more energetic, resourceful states. Life is so much more fulfilling when you are able to create the feelings you desire, which in turn create more positive thinking. The key to this simple skill is to become aware of the power of words.

When you describe how you feel, use power language – positive, descriptive, and exciting words. For me, instead of saying I am a pretty good dad or an involved dad, I say to myself, "I am the most outstanding, terrific, and caring dad in the world." Whether I actually am or not is less important than becoming more aware of my actions, which makes living up to my assertion a more likely possibility.

When we use powerful words to describe what we think of our present situation, we are more likely to continue to think positively. This is good for our physical and mental health. What we think and say has an impact on how we feel, which in turn influences our thinking. The positive feedback loop creates a positive reality, just as a negative cycle will feed on itself destructively.

Now what is the lesson here for us all from Sparkle Kitty? How we present ourselves to the world impacts our thinking. Events do not define who we are; how we act defines who we are, which influences how we think!

## Self-Acceptance is a Skill; Self-Esteem is the Habit of Using It

One of the main benefits of positive thinking is self-acceptance, but it is also the first step. There can be no positive thinking without self-acceptance. As your self-acceptance grows, you develop self-esteem.

I think of self-acceptance as the ability to create positive thinking about one's strong *and* weak points, and doing so habitually results in positive self-esteem. Self-acceptance helps you to keep good thoughts in mind, as well as project them. There are many people training others how to think positively. All these trainers say they have the plum of knowledge that one needs to think more positively. They all claim to hold the key to the "ingénue" mind. The fact is that the transmission of strategies alone does not always help the individual. What does help is the *awareness* that what they think will take shape in their experience.

Once we realize self-acceptance is key, we are ready to learn the strategies of positive thinking. It doesn't take a guru like Stephen Covey to tell us that for the past fifty years our society has been focusing on how to do things faster and more easily.

Holocaust survivor and psychiatrist Viktor Frankl wrote in *Man's Search for Meaning* that one of his most powerful discoveries was an inner sense of freedom while the Nazis were doing medical experiments on him. One of the main themes of his writing is that we always have final choice. In his case, he believed they could have his body, but never his mind. We can project positive thoughts under the most extreme conditions, and we can determine how we will respond and act. We have free will to create the thoughts we want; thoughts that are ours, and can never be taken from us.

Even for persons suffering from obsessive-compulsive disorder – an anxiety disorder that may have origins in the individual's brain chemistry, and may cause them to suffer from repeating unwanted thoughts or actions – intention is always pristine. So even if your mind strays, your heart's intentions speak true.

Many have taken on the societal belief that positive thinking is of little real value. Show me anyone who was a world leader who did not have a strong belief in what they could do!

Being curious about the source of Emily's positivism, I asked her why she always says she is "just great." She answered, "I want to be just great, so that all of my friends will want to play with me. No one will want to play with me if I am not."

Popularity may not be everything, but at five, she'd already hit on something that is absolutely true. Would you want to be with someone who was not "just great"? There are exceptions, but most of us prefer to be with happy people. We are attracted to positive thinking, and will gravitate towards it when it is present. Unfortunately, too many times we are drawn into unnecessarily negative interchanges.

When I started to think about Sparkle Kitty's observation, I was struck by the seed of maturity it contained. I remember wondering at God's mysterious ways. The universe sends teachers in many forms. My new master had taken the form of a five-year-old. According to Sparkle Kitty, to be able to think you are just great, you need to have positive thoughts in your head the vast majority of the time.

**Tips for Building Self-Acceptance**

1. Expect that you will make mistakes; it is part of the deal of living as a human being. It cannot be avoided. No one is perfect, and nowhere does it say you need to be.

2. Life has challenges, and so will you. There is no perfect time for a life challenge such as death of a loved one, loss of employment or other major stresses in life. You did not do anything to deserve them – change is inevitable.

3. Anger is hardly a guarantee for success or getting what you want. Using it on yourself or others will often work for the short-term, but with time the cost will increase. Anger is not a way to get what you want, or like who you are. Anger involves a loss of control and is a scary way to live.

4. Be positive in your thoughts for others so you can be positive for yourself. What we think about others is what we will think about ourselves.

5. Accept the concept of improving your self-esteem. Nowhere is there evidence that you are not allowed to like who you are and enjoy life.

6. Let your *soul* shine through. We can't all be on the cover of Rolling Stone. Do not make body image the only criterion that determines self-acceptance. This is an illusion that too many of us have bought into.

7. Practice what you preach. Many of us coach others better than we live life ourselves. Become a role model for yourself, and live life how you know it can be.

8. Live life in the present. That is where you are, and from there you prepare for the future.

9. Promote to yourself who you are, not what you have done. It is important to be focused on who you are, not what you are. People can lose stuff, but you can't lose yourself if you know who you are.

10. Be clear on your values and your personal life goals. Monitor how you talk to yourself. Say only good things. When you slip, forgive, forget, and move on. The key to train your brain is to remind yourself you are a good person the way you are. Learn to like who you are.

11. Slow down and take care of your mind and your body. Treat them with respect.

12. Do not use chemicals to enhance your mind. Do not rob your body of the food and nutrition it needs. Treat yourself the way you would want to be treated if you had the time to do it. The key to making time is to schedule it. There are no shortcuts.

As a society, we all need to spend time developing our self-esteem, so we can better like who we are. The best start is to practice this core life principle daily, like Sparkle Kitty does. Be aware, adults, that when we don't infringe on a child's self-esteem, it will stay intact. *All children are born with healthy self-esteem.* It is only through time and exposure to our adult society do they unlearn it!

This is why school systems so desperately need to offer self-esteem training – to remind children who they are, and help support them so they don't give up. They need training to offset all the negative messages they receive. We must also teach self-esteem to adults in the professional world. Daniel Goleman (1995) says emotional intelligence determines 90 percent of a person's success.

**Tips for Enhancing Self-Esteem**

1. Read lots of materials written for the purpose of enhancing self-esteem. Go to any bookstore or library and you will find a great deal of information on this topic in the personal development section.

2. Learn how to say no to all the garbled and contradictory messages carried in the media. We all have our own body type: endomorphic (heavy set), ectomorphic (thin), and mesomorphic (muscular). We can be healthy, but we can't fool genes. Create your own picture of who you want to be in regard to a realistic body image. *Set a norm of health, not perfection!*

3. Develop a strong support group. Yes, having a support group takes time and effort. Invest in yourself by making time for others.

4. Journal daily, so you can measure the facts of life and avoid the opinions. It is your life, so it must be worth recording. I also suggest you continue to read books on self-esteem as part of your growth.
5. Be honest with yourself and others. Lying only makes things seem better. In the end, dishonesty will truly destroy your self-esteem.
6. Only stay in situations that support your self-concept. Get out of abusive and painful situations quickly. There is no proof that time will improve how you perceive abuse and pain. If these are present, you must get away until you are sure they are totally gone.
7. Set clear boundaries on what you will and will not accept from others, and stick to them. Be very assertive on your personal moral standards.
8. Learn to accept a compliment, and to praise yourself out loud to others. It is okay to be proud of what you achieve in life.

**Self-Affirmation**

No matter how small the task, Sparkle Kitty always wants to make sure that she feels good about doing it. When it's done, she will always affirm herself. She wants Sherrie and me to acknowledge how well she did as well. Children who do not receive a lot of time or positive feedback from their parents may find it difficult to think they are okay as they grow into adults. Some do okay on their own by watching others, although unfortunately more do not. Children are easy to reinforce for positive thinking, because they all have it at birth. We just need to let it grow, and remind them of what they already know as they grow into adults.

Value development theorist Morris Massey (1993) believed the core values of a human being are installed in the "imprint era" between birth and age seven. The ability to think positively is inborn, but by the age of six we have all been programmed with regard to our core life values. Because values act as lenses through which we perceive the world, they affect how positively we perceive it.

Personality filters, in particular, affect your learning style – how you process information. The Meyers-Briggs test is one of the more popular measures to help you assess the way you interact with the world. The test measures your interactions on four different spectrums – in terms of being introverted/extroverted, feeling/thinking, sensory/intuitive, and perceptive/judgmental.

Martin Seligam, president of the American Psychological Association, wrote a great deal on the issue of optimism and pessimism, and created many self-evaluation techniques. But no matter which end of the spectrum you're coming from, to become an optimist, you have to become aware of your own thinking.

It may help you learn to think positively if you learn about your personality.

**What is your personality?**

Every human being has a unique assortment of traits that form his or her personality. If you can imagine a stereo's equalizer board, you've got the picture. Imagine each sliding button represents a personality trait. Each of the approximately 180 known personality traits can be rated on a percent scale, so it's easy to see how much variance there can be. No two people have the same combination of traits, and it would be difficult enough to find two people with the same degree of a given trait.

The field of psychology has attempted to classify personality by cluster because there would be too many specifics otherwise.

I have identified 20 personality traits that support positive thinking. These traits are also useful in developing the other childmind attributes. I suggest that you review them, and test yourself to see which ones are already going for you.

**Twenty Personality Traits That Help People Think Positively**

1. Flexibility – the ability to adjust to life challenges.
2. Curiosity – interest in what is possible.
3. Anticipation (foresight) – looking ahead, so you are ready.
4. Persistence – never giving up on yourself.
5. Determination and Commitment – knowing you'll get there if you stay on course.
6. Ethics and Morals – making responsible decisions.
7. Empathy and Compassion – awareness of the impact of your actions on others.
8. Loyalty – staying true to what is important to you.
9. Ambition – desire to do the best you can; willingness to grow and change.
10. Passion – zest for life.
11. Independence – ability to think for yourself.
12. Self-awareness – being a witness to your thoughts, feelings and actions.
13. Optimism – ability to see positive outcomes.

14. Humility – the ability to serve; to put others before yourself; and allow others to have their ego strong in your presence.
15. Generosity – willingness to give to others.
16. Gratitude – ability to be grateful for what you have.
17. Patience – ability to delay gratification, and wait for what you want in a relaxed manner.
18. Honesty – to tell the truth to yourself and others.
19. Composure – ability to stay calm, cool, and collected in challenging times.
20. Self-worth – knowing you are okay and worthwhile.

Read through this list twice, to self-evaluate which traits you demonstrate regularly, and which ones need work.

Understanding that we all filter the world a little differently is important. No two people will create the exact same reality. Become aware of this, and be careful not to judge others as you progress through life. No one can be like you or act exactly like you. The same rule holds true for you – you cannot be exactly the same as someone else. What we can do is learn which of our personality traits are helpful, and dampen or extinguish the hurtful ones. Become aware of your filters and how they influence your thinking. Become proactive in this endeavour. If you are able to keep it up, your journey of self-awareness is under way.

Self-awareness grows out of thought-by-thought and feeling-by-feeling attention to your responses. If you've ever celebrated life's little moments, you probably know how difficult it is to even notice them with negative thoughts crowding your mind. When you are outside and the air is crisp and the sky is blue, the leaves and flowers could be in bloom, or changing colour, or under a blanket of snow. The season or time of day does not matter. The activity in which you are engaged is also secondary. You could be walking, driving, or doing yard work. A warm, peaceful feeling comes over you. This reward comes from your awareness of the now – what the Buddhist calls mindfulness. But you don't have to be a Buddhist to celebrate the little moments. The only way to have this experience is with a present mind. Positive thinking will help you train a present mind – a mind that will allow you to accept the world, see its true beauty, and be one with it.

I've met a lot of people who do not accept or pay attention to these moments that happen every day of our lives. We are what we think, and we have no other reality than to become what we think. What we think we are, we will become!

I have learned that the key to life is to first learn how to think positively about who you are. It is a good idea to define yourself positively first. If you cannot do this, you cannot think positively about others or the world. There are no shortcuts or magic solutions to this. The first step is to become aware of the fact that we cannot move until we are aware of the power of our daily thinking. Napoleon Hill's book *Think and Grow Rich* contains some timeless wisdom. My favourite, his thesis, is that "a man will become what he thinks."

This principle can be self-taught, learned from peers, a coach, books, religion or a great movie. We can learn it any time, any place. The learning curve may be years or seconds. The truth is that we all started out with the ability to think positively – the secret is keeping it up. We are all energy forms, and can shape that energy at light speed if we so desire. For me, change is like a light switch on the wall. I can turn it on or leave it off. Both are my choice. Both require action. Sparkle Kitty has reminded me of the joy of having the light switch on, and how wonderful it is to see the world through a positive filter.

Sparkle Kitty has reminded me that analyzing life to death is not the best use of our energy. She lives life in the moment. She only sees positive, and is conditioned to want to think positive. What could we learn if we all did this in our lives? What if we could all think positive, and say we are *just great*? What if you just turned your light switch on and said, I am willing to think 95 percent positive thoughts? What if the world did this together, and believed in this idea? What kind of world would we live in? We may never always have positive thoughts, although if each of us were to focus on producing positive thoughts, the results would be outstanding for us all!

The fact is, we cannot wait for the world to do this. We cannot afford to wait for others to do it first; we need to follow the lead of our children. We need to understand that only we can do it for ourselves, and only for ourselves. Everyone else is not our job. We can support, coach, guide, and lead, but we cannot change others – only they can. It is neither our right nor choice. You can lead a horse to water, but it's up to the horse to drink. The same is true for human beings. Of course, we can be influenced and helped, although the choice to accept help is also the individual's. When we live with this principle, we are being truly positive role models.

**Is Image a Booster or a Buster?**

Sadly, what stands in the way of many people becoming self-directed or self-realized is hang-ups about appearance. A large section of the population obtains a great deal of its self-esteem from external looks. We do live in a cosmetic world. What is more powerful to a man than a drop-dead beautiful woman who has everything in the right place? The unfortunate and sad truth is a wealthy drop-dead beautiful woman has a great deal of power in a man's world. Why? Does a beautiful woman with self-esteem have power? If she does, how did she get it? What was the benchmark? Despite the women's rights movement, I do not see that this has changed as much as it should – we still put a great deal of emphasis on *looks*.

The number one surgery in North America is breast augmentation. Why? Because we have set the mark that a female with curves is more appealing and valued. We all know that beauty is in the eyes of the beholder. Unfortunately, too many of us have never found our internal beauty. Looks are only skin deep. I know many beautiful women who are lonely because no man thought he was good enough to ask them out. I think it is fine to want to look good, although we need to learn to accept our limitations, and like who we are. If we take care of ourselves and live a healthy lifestyle, we can balance our inner and outer beauty.

Look at the numbers of anorexic and bulimic teens in our society. Look at the age of onset for these illnesses. Where are these young teenagers learning the message to be thin equals beauty? There is obviously a message being sent that is leading many people to develop the belief that body image is a major factor in determining if others will accept us. Many people are conditioned to believe they need others' approval for acceptance, thus they will not accept themselves until others accept them first. This is why we need to learn to develop this and the other core life principles. The main judge we have to contend with in the here and now is us.

Sparkle Kitty is so beautiful. At age seven, she looks perfect to me. When I say perfect, I mean healthy and happy. When I say healthy, I mean her heart is working more effectively since the operation she had in 1995. My frame of measurement of beauty for her is that she is healthy and happy. Wouldn't it be better to evaluate yourself against the criteria of happiness and health, instead of the cover of *Playboy* or *Cosmopolitan*? Sparkle Kitty loves who she is – just ask her, she will tell you herself. I very often ask adults in my personal development workshops, "How many of you got up this morning and said, 'Damn, I'm good-looking – inside and out!' "

Unfortunately a lot of people equate liking yourself to egoism. On the other hand, if you do not like yourself, it could make you sick – and sooner or later you are going to end up in your doctor's office, either because you are depressed or have developed some type of psychosomatic illness.

The continuum below indicates that the farther you are on the left you are more confident, and less concerned about others' points of view. You would have an elevated sense of self-worth, and would have a difficult time accepting rejection. On the right side of the continuum, a person with zero egoism would have very low self-esteem, and would be much more likely to suffer from depression and other kinds of illness. We all move back and forth on this continuum, however, for wellness and health, it is important to stay out of the extreme ends.

**Excessive Egoism** --------------------NORMAL ZONE------------------------- **Zero Egoism**

Can we make this any more confusing for human beings? Were you ever taught how to remind yourself as you get older to continue to like who you are? All children once liked themselves. Only through interaction with adults do they learn how to not like who they are. Some say children are cruel to each other. Where do they learn this?

How much training did you get in school to learn to like yourself? Ten years as a school consultant showed me our education system does not offer nearly enough training in self-esteem, especially among the older grades. Meanwhile, we're learning lots of other things that we will quickly forget, and never use. Learning to like who we are, and being okay with ourselves may be ultimately more important than academics. In reality, it's not an either/or debate – we need both kinds of training. How many people do you know who really like who they are? What percentage of the population likes themselves?

The principle of self-esteem should be more than a starting point. How many children start school liking themselves, and leave school with poor self-esteem? Most of these graduates start school thinking they are 9 or 10 out of 10, and leave school believing they are 6s – feeling mediocre and barely passing in the self-like category! So the best they can give others is a 5 – they will never be able to give more than they have, nor are they able to role model more than they believe they are.

Look at the hard facts on how many children compensate for not liking themselves. Many compensate by using drugs. Some can no longer stand the pain, and kill themselves. The number one killer of youth is drug-related car accidents (mostly alcohol), and number two is suicide. Is this a problem in our society? You bet! There is no bigger one I know of than youth not liking who they are. This is a core life principle that we all *must* have in place. To get it, we must practice it and develop it.

If we want our children to have self-esteem, we need to ensure teachers have the support to develop theirs. I understand the argument that parents need to be more involved, and that too much is left to the schools. But adults, hear me, all of you: self-esteem requires as much training and skill-development as reading and writing!

I work a great deal with teachers in schools. One of my concerns is the low self-concept of many teachers. Teachers are the role models for our children. Phrases like "positive learning environment" and "classroom management" are buzzwords in today's schools. However, if you like yourself, and have rapport with children, you will have very few concerns and challenges. The best teachers are the ones who like who they are, and like the children. They can do this because they have a strong self-esteem. Constant power struggles with students are, in my mind, a symptom of low self-esteem.

Teachers with classroom management concerns need to start with themselves. The same principle holds true for any profession. Professional coaching is one of the fastest growing professions, only because of the perceived need. Many do not want to wait until they are mentally ill to get help. They want to find and keep their edge. They see coaching as a way to enhance and maintain their self-esteem so they move farther in life. I see coaching as a proactive way for people to continue to learn and grow. The ultimate goal is being able to accept and like who they are, so they can achieve all their dreams.

There are so many how-to books and workshops – for everything from making millions to overcoming addictions. They are all well intended, I am sure. But without question, if you do not have *self-rapport*, you will have difficulty developing rapport with others, and your self-esteem will lag.

In simple terms, self-rapport is very similar to self-esteem – with one difference. Self-esteem is the feeling you have after you have performed whatever you are doing – when you tie your laces for the first time, or learn to ride your bike. It is how you feel about yourself based on what you have done! On the Children's Television Workshop cartoon *DragonTales*, a band of friendly dragon characters wears dragon badges which light up when they have faced a personal challenge. Each dragon has a different challenge – Ord is afraid of the dark; Cassie is shy; and two-headed dragon twins Zak, quiet and orderly, and Wheezie, noisy and flamboyant, must learn to get along!

Only you can determine what your dragon badge is! Self-rapport is a core skill that will enhance the development of your self-esteem. We need the tool of knowing we can influence our thinking. Self-rapport is the mindset of becoming accepting of yourself, so you can make the journey of developing your self-esteem. It is ingrained in the principle of positive thinking.

**Tips for Creating Positive Thinking**

1. Understand that there are no givens – and this doesn't mean we should be fearful. If we don't like things as they are, we can change them.
2. Accept the present, and celebrate time with your family and children and alone.
3. Stop and become aware of the power of positive thinking. For seven days, do an exercise where you try to think only positive. At the end of the week, notice the joy and power of positive thinking.
4. Define what is important. Too many people worry about what is not important, and forget what they already have is important.
5. Believe that good thoughts lead to a good life. The path of happiness starts with awareness. A few tips: a) if you do not have a good thought, get rid of it, and find a good thought before you speak; b) when you talk about others, only talk in the positive, do not talk behind others' backs – it creates ill will; c) practice thinking positive things about people who challenge you; d) if you make a mistake, correct

it quickly; e) watch your progress daily as your awareness and positive thinking grow.

6. Start your positive journey now. There is no one you can depend on more than *you* to get what you want. Do not wait around for free lunches.
7. Be clear that life is never defined by one event. There is always another opportunity. Life is a journey with a beginning, middle, and end.
8. In life there are no roadblocks – we only need to accept the detours. The way to make this so is to first choose how you want to think, and thereby view the world.
9. Mistakes happen, so learn from them. Do not allow yourself to become stunned and stuck in negativity. If you get off track, just forgive and forget, and start making your thoughts positive again. Take an inventory to learn your values and your personality traits and type.
10. When you get what you want, remember to enjoy it. The process of writing down daily what you have is a good way for you to find the magic in your life. This will start to train your brain to become positive.

For further tips on positive thinking, become familiar with Glasser's *Choice Theory*, and the work of Albert Ellis, author of *Rational Emotive Behavioral Therapy*. Both these works are great educational tools. Go to a bookstore or search the Internet to find their ideas.

Jim Rohn teaches the best intervention is to invest in your self-development. What is your happiness worth to you?

I believe this world was originated from a single thought. You have the power to create what you want with your thoughts. The option is yours to turn your focus inward, and think of the power of pure positivism. Things happen to us all. Some of them are worse than others. To move ahead in life, we must get to the point where we are able to move beyond self-created negative thinking. The path for this is awareness of all our thinking.

Sparkle Kitty has given me a chance to wake up and smell not just the roses, but all the other beautiful flowers in life's garden. My outlook is defined one thought at a time. Creating a positive outlook on the world is like writing a book – one word at a time. We create our lives one thought at a time.

Good things take time, and we cannot expect life to change overnight. We can take the action to start the change, and then let go of the outcome for a while. We need to

# 4 The Power of Hope 65

make the priority of self-esteem development, but we need to be patient and diligent. When you can work on your self-esteem, you will, through effort, be able to get everything you need, if not what you want.

*In closing . . .*

We are the only ones who can determine who we are and what our lives will be. This core life principle is a major one. We will be much happier and healthier if we take the time and effort to develop these principles. We can't afford *not* to take the time. The pay-off when we like ourselves unconditionally is that we are better able to accept others unconditionally. When we do not like who we are, we find it harder to like others the way we really could. Don't implode like a black hole. Become your own star, and let yourself shine brightly. This will help guide you on your journey.

Sparkle Kitty Coaching: It takes practice to like who we are!

## Sparkle Action

The activities listed below will help you study this chapter, and obtain the learning from it. The way to enhance your knowledge is by studying and self-reflection, and then practice.

1. On a scale of 1 (low) and 10 (high), how much are you already living this childmind principle today? _____

2. List three points from this chapter that may have had special significance for you:

    a) _____

    b) _____

    c) _____

3. How will this principle help you in each of the five *life balance* areas?
   In the space provided, be specific about each area:

   Health: _____

   Self: _____

   Relationships: _____

   Career: _____

   Money: _____

4. What is one insight you believe you need to act on?

   _____

   What is your action plan?

   _____

   List the steps here:

   _____

   _____

   _____

# Chapter 5
# The Power of Imagination

*"Little Rosie is here!" – Sparkle Kitty*

LITTLE ROSIE is a fairy, two inches tall, who has been our imaginary houseguest since Emily learned to talk.

After an extended leave of absence last year, Emily informed us, a few months ago, that Little Rosie was back.

Emily can describe this blue-eyed fairy in detail – she has curly blond hair and almost always wears a pink or red dress. Little Rosie flies, really quickly, in and out of the windows while we're driving, and sleeps in the crook of a bow on Emily's headboard.

Little Rosie sets a good example. Her counterpart – Big Rosie – is not so well behaved; but between the two of them, Emily is able to work out a great deal of inner conflict.

Little Rosie and Big Rosie have been a very real part of Emily's childhood, but at the same time, Emily knows they aren't real.

For me, Little Rosie is something of a symbol for Emily's limitless creative imagination.

There are several definitions for imagination. The one we all think of evokes a sort of inner movie screen: the faculty of reproducing or recombining images stored in memory from association or experience. But imagination also refers to the ability to meet and resolve difficulties.

Children often use play to work out their personal struggles. Sparkle Kitty, for example, being a normal seven-year-old, will refuse when Sherrie and I ask her to clean up her room. This choice often results in our enforcing a boundary, and handing her a consequence – a "time-out." Like most children, she may not think of it as a choice until she's in the time-out. This situation, of course, creates an internal conflict.

I find it amazing that when the dust settles and she calms down, she will use the two Rosies and any number of Beanie Babies to work out what happened, and learn from it.

Children resolve a great deal of pain this way. Sparkle Kitty also uses play to change her focus. By becoming engrossed in something else she enjoys, she finds relief. Play, then, presents many opportunities for problem solving.

Children can often come up with a way through whatever is bothering them. They can forget very quickly, and stay out of the past, with the exception of those in abusive and other extreme situations. They know how to live in the present, and get over day-to-day disappointments very quickly. This is why children rarely hold grudges against parents who make mistakes. Creativity allows them to find other meanings for what has happened. Flexibility makes it possible for children to forgive, and find the good in what they want to. Adults can learn a lesson from this. Creativity helps us avoid getting stuck in negative thought patterns. Many of us hold grudges for many years, simply because we cannot find a way to see the situation differently.

People who are able to get through or over what I call *life potholes* are better at making new beginnings for themselves. It's easy to feel as if there is no way out when things aren't going our way. But creativity helps us find new choices – new ways of overcoming obstacles, or avoiding them altogether. Creativity allows us to find new ways to build relationships – which we know can be a source of conflict, as well as happiness. Creativity allows us, according to Viktor Frankl, the privilege to carry out our ultimate freedom: our human will.

The fact is that with time alone many of these perceived potholes fix themselves. We turn many life challenges into bigger ones when we focus only on the problems. Creativity is the agent that will help us find a path to the future we want. We need to believe that if we don't have the right answer at the time of need, we will figure it out. Creativity cannot be forced – it must be allowed. We need to relax, allow our creative system to work, and also allow that a great many of the ideas we come up with may not prove workable. If we can embrace our efforts without judgment, our creative system will continue to produce. Eventually, a viable solution will almost always show up – or be brought to us from someone else. We need to *ask and wait,* and the answers will come.

Give Sparkle Kitty a problem, and she will give you an answer. To solve a problem, we need to take action, and detach from the outcome. Failure is an opportunity for learning. When he was faced with an obstacle, Alexander Graham Bell made a common practice of asking children what they thought. He knew that children don't put limitations on their vision of what is possible, and they never judge an idea; they just offer it.

Brian Tracy, the famous business coach, claims each of us comes up with on average, one idea per year that would make us millionaires. If only we would act on these ideas, and follow them through. But most people do not trust their ability to create. The inner brilliance is there in many of us, but lies dormant for most of our lives – and in some cases, never wakes up. The power of creativity we had as children is with us still; we just need to give it permission to grow – and thereby acknowledge our true genius. Yes, it may take time to reassert itself, but with a little conviction on your part, creativity won't let you down.

In this society, we are taught to judge our ideas so well that most of us suppress our ability to be creative. Unfortunately, some of us missed developing our creativity when we had the most available opportunities, but it's never too late to change the way we *think*.

The ability to solve problems is a fundamental skill that combines both hemispheres of the brain – your analytical modes of thinking as well as your intuitive ones. We need whole-brained creativity to generate the new ideas our life challenges demand.

According to the research on brain hemisphere function, each side of the brain has evolved to perform particular tasks. The left brain manages logical, sequential, rational, analytical, objective, and detail-oriented thinking. This is the side that allows us to, for example, organize words for reading and writing, to distinguish, discriminate, and classify. The right brain is intuitive, random, abstract, holistic, subjective, and whole-oriented. It is concerned with spatial concepts and non-verbal expression – "creativity" as we ordinarily think of it. This is the side that allows us to gesture, draw pictures, interpret music, and understand geometry theorems.

Most individuals have a distinct preference for one style of thinking, in varying degrees. In general, schools have tended to promote left-brain modes of thinking, while downplaying right-brain modes – especially in the recent era of budget cuts to art and music, the so-called "frills."

In the classical and medieval world, music was considered an important part of a balanced education. The Greeks and Romans identified music as a relative of mathematics, geometry, and astronomy – one of four essential abstract languages (the "quadrivium") for the right brain.

The left brain was given logic/reason, dialectic, and grammar for food – the "trivium."

But creative expression accompanies the development of both sides of the brain, as youngsters learn how to communicate feelings and ideas through many media: the written word, colours on canvas, scientific trial, mathematical solution, philosophical argument, musical composition, mechanical innovation – even financial plans!

Writers, like other artists, must use both halves of their brains. They must create things (right-brain), and they must organize them (left-brain) into communicable ideas. Great scientists, like Albert Einstein, and more recently, Canadian biogeneticist Johan Peninger, rely on right-brain intuition before applying left-brain method and analysis. Peninger's research "hunches" on the human genome have paid off in osteoporosis and cancer breakthroughs. Albert Einstein was motivated by sound intuition based on penetrating observation and painstaking assessment of data. He had an ability from childhood to understand difficult concepts.

Does this mean most people in our society are quite logical, and not very creative? They may think so. But the very word "think" is a left-brain way of describing the situation, which, with awareness, people can change.

Statistics gathered by American artist and philosopher Harry Hilson show that almost all children rank high in creativity before entering school. According to Hilson, only 10 percent of U.S. children rank high in creativity by age seven, and by the time they reach adulthood, only 2 percent rank high in creativity.

The power of a young child's imagination is so grand I wonder how we forget to be creative. Unfortunately, too many children get conditioned to allow adults to solve their problems. They emerge from childhood lacking an entire skill set. All children start out with the ability to problem-solve, although many lose it when they interface with the adult world.

Before children learn to read, we rely heavily on art and music to teach them. Perhaps once logic and verbal capacity are developed to the very great degree they seem called upon for use in our society, the earlier abilities atrophy. Or perhaps we haven't factored in the effects of television watching on brain development, as children "evolve" toward more sedentary adults.

Play itself offers many learning opportunities.

Young children who need to entertain themselves play! Problem solved!

Children at play aren't interested in boundaries, real or imaginary.

Ashby's Law of Requisite Variety states that the mechanism with the greatest amount of flexibility and creativity will lead the system. The famous children's story *Green Eggs and Ham*, by Dr. Seuss (Theodore Geisel) is a wonderful illustration of the systematic persistence of the creative mind. Persistent application of small change, will, over time, chart a course of dynamic change.

I sum up creative problem-solving this way:

**F**ollow your intuition. Initiate every idea you can.

**L**et your conscience guide you. Be clear about your intentions

**O**pen to the universe, but consider the pros and cons.

**W**ork. Remember, creativity takes effort and patience. Stay focused.

The skill of being able to act with spontaneity is basic, if you are to take advantage of the opportunities you need when faced with a life pothole. Zig Ziglar describes fear as one of the biggest blocks to allowing a person to take action and move beyond their present situation. We all have to address these challenges in our lives, and the only way is through action. Below is a plan of how you can take on your life potholes in a proactive manner.

**Overcoming Life Potholes:**

- You want to enjoy life, not just survive it. Do not settle for not succeeding unless you want others to settle for your not succeeding!
- All life challenges take perseverance. Get the word *quit* out of your vocabulary, and you are halfway there.
- No plan was charted out perfectly the first time. Understand that you will need to be creative in solving potholes. Do not worry about the perfect road – take the middle road, and just be focused on getting there.
- Be true to yourself – it is imperative not to give up your values to get ahead!
- Success is an outcome. Go past success in your mind's eye, and look at how your actions are defining you as a person. Your accomplishments aren't just another victory; they are part of you.
- Ensure you are solving potholes in all five areas of your life (money, career, relationships, self, and health). The ultimate goal is total life balance. Be aware of your focuses and whether you are spending all your energy solving challenges. Do not allow these potholes to grow unattended.
- We are all human beings doing the best we can. Ensure you have compassion and empathy for others when you are looking for your solutions.
- Forget the word *try*. Train your brain not to ask why you should do something, or you won't get past starting.
- The best way to solve a life pothole is to avoid falling into one in the first place – the proactive is always preferable to the reactive. We need to take responsibility for our actions, and understand that we always have the freedom to choose our own path. Not making a choice is our choice. Believing we have no choice is our choice. Be progressive, not regressive in your actions. Look for solutions, not band-aids!
- Forget the past and look to the future when looking to find a new way. Only go to the past if there is healthy and positive learning there for you.

Having a structured format to help you address your concerns is helpful to focus and facilitate your creativity. I suggest you look at the brief problem-solving model below to help you work through life potholes. To use this model, take your life challenge, and work it through the steps one at a time.

# 5 THE POWER OF IMAGINATION

**A Guide to Solving Life Potholes**

1. *Define the Pothole*
   a) What is your challenge?
   b) How is it manifesting in your life? (e.g., if worry is a problem, how are you worrying?)
   c) How do you know it is a problem?
   d) Clearly define your problem in one or two sentences.
   e) What are the consequences if you do not solve it?

2. *Review Actions Taken to Solve Pothole*
   a) What have you done in the past to solve a similar situation successfully?
   b) What are your friends and family telling you to do?
   c) What is your gut telling you?
   d) What might you have to give up for a solution?
   e) If you continue to live life with this challenge, will you be okay?

3. *Define your Desired Outcome*
   a) What is a reasonable solution to this pothole?
   b) If you do not know, suppose for a moment you did know. What would be a reasonable goal?
   c) Imagine you had a magic wand and could do anything to solve the situation. What would you do?
   d) Pretend you are three weeks out and the problem is solved. What actions, thinking, and emotions got you to this point?
   e) What do you know you really want to happen?

4. *Taking Actions to Move Through the Pothole*
   a) What can you do today that is a start? Be specific with the actions you are going to take.
   b) Make a plan that is S.I.M.P.L.E.: Simple, Immediate, Measurable, Plausible, Legal, and Ethical.
   c) All solutions start with a beginning: action. Then you need to work through the middle, where you learn what else you need to know, and the ending is when you can see you are moving away from the pothole.

We are all faced with life problems. There is no one solution I know that will solve all life issues. There is no god in boxes out there. All we have is our experiences, our personality traits, our values, our life principles, our will, and ourselves. Above are tips on how to solve life challenges. Our childmind is needed when faced with a true life problem. However, only we can define what constitutes a problem for us. Some problems are universally obvious; but regardless of the problem, creativity is key to the solution – and finding a way to enjoy life to the full.

**Ten Tips to Increase your Creativity**

1. For one week, stop judging what you – and others – do.

2. Allow yourself to experiment. The key is not to evaluate if it is working until you are doing. Too many experiments are stopped before they have ever been started.

3. Join a Master Mind group. These groups have sprung from Hill's idea that when two people team up with the same goal, anything is possible. (Read any book written by Napoleon Hill.)

4. Take a workshop in creativity so you can learn exercises on how to enhance you creativity.

5. Write your ideas down. Many of us forget our solutions. Have a pen and paper with you at all times, even by your bed. Get in the habit of writing or taping your thoughts.

6. Start to acknowledge yourself daily with how flexible and creative you are. Do this daily with intent for 90 days and enjoy the outcomes. Please reread Dr. Seuss's children's story *Green Eggs and Ham* for an excellent reminder of the power of creativity.

7. Ask your children for their advice, and listen for the answer between the lines – listen *carefully*.

8. Accept failure as nothing more than feedback on the need to redefine the path or a signpost that a new path awaits.

# 5 The Power of Imagination

9. When looking for creativity, try to see your life in terms of the problem already being solved, and the benefits you have in place. Think in terms of how things are now in the future. The idea is to be there in the future, and to be in a good state, so that your mind is stress-free. At this point, you will be able to see more clearly the path that got you there. From this, you are able to figure out the steps for your success and solution.
10. Creativity is nothing more than the permission to think without boundaries. Give yourself this permission, and believe it! Become aware of your true creativity.

One of my favourite television shows when I was growing up was MacGyver, which was taped in British Columbia. MacGyver was a master both at using his imagination and putting basic laws of science to work. He knew he was able to think outside the box. He blew up the box! He did not allow the environment to determine what he was going to be able to do. When it looked like he was done for good, he would take a piece of gum, a beer can, a wire, and a box of soap detergent to make a bomb and foil his attacker.

*In closing . . .*

We all have the power of creativity and imagination. Each of us possesses these things, we just need to let them out. We need to believe we have the solutions in us, and not be afraid to make mistakes. Edison said mistakes are a victory of learning. When we become aware of the power of creativity, we will see life challenges not as gaping potholes ready to swallow us, but as opportunities for new beginnings. As with any skill, creativity and problem-solving take time and practice. The great news is that there are no limitations to what a human mind can create. And yes, that includes you!

> **Sparkle Kitty Coaching:**
> I use play; it works. It helps me; it will work for you.

## Sparkle Action

The activities listed below will help you study this chapter, and obtain the learning from it. The way to enhance your knowledge is by studying and self-reflection, and then practice.

1. On a scale of 1 (low) and 10 (high), how much are you already living this childmind principle today? _____

2. List three points from this chapter that may have had special significance for you:

    a) _____

    b) _____

    c) _____

3. How will this principle help you in each of the five *life balance* areas?
   In the space provided, be specific about each area:

   Health: _____

   Self: _____

   Relationships: _____

   Career: _____

   Money: _____

4. What is one insight you believe you need to act on?

   _____

   What is your action plan?

   _____

   List the steps here:

   _____

   _____

   _____

# Chapter 6

# The Power of Learning

*"Can I ask you a question?" – Sparkle Kitty*

OF COURSE Sparkle Kitty can ask me a question! The pope *is* Polish!

"Can I ask you a question?" isn't just a question. Sparkle Kitty knows, of course, that she is perfectly able to ask questions, even before she pipes up. And I know that she is perfectly able to ask questions. . . . I mean, who would we be kidding? What she is really doing, when she says this, is warning me, a) that I'd better be listening, because b) there is about to be an interrogation.

Have you ever noticed how a kid can keep up their end of a two-hour conversation by asking "Why?" every time you pause for air? If you saw Macaulay Culkin and John Candy in the movie "Uncle Buck," you will remember the "interview" which concludes with Culkin saying, "I'm a kid, it's my job."

Sparkle Kitty is the Queen Bee of Questions, the Master Popper of the Why. Almost every second noise she makes is a question. We are all born with the instinct to fill in the blanks of life, to worry the "whys" like a dog with a bone.

It amazes me how persistent Sparkle Kitty can be. And sponge-like. She wants to soak up every droplet of information and experience available. At the end of the day, she is full, goes to sleep – to wring out, I guess – and awakens to sop up another day's worth of knowledge.

As an educator, I know there is a significant portion of our population who find learning tiresome. In particular, people whose attempts to learn – or just be themselves – are ridiculed, may lose their sense of wonder.

When Emily first started at Coldbrook School, after we moved back to Canada, I asked her what she thought of her new teacher, Ramona Jennex-Williams. She told me, "I love her voice. I could just close my eyes and listen to her teaching me and learn what she's talking about because I love her voice."

Unfortunately for too many children, the public school system has been reduced – and reduces them – to basic survival. When these same students started school, however, they *liked it*. Youngsters from a stable, safe home will invariably enter school with a passion to learn. All children are sponges, but for some reason a great number of them lose their passion to learn.

What happens? Many get turned off in school because learning is not seen as need-fulfilling or fun as obtaining peer acceptance, or immersing oneself in sports, hobbies or video games. Also, a large group of the population has learning concerns which have been labelled dyslexia and/or attention deficit disorder. I was diagnosed in both categories, and it's my opinion that we are over-diagnosing both.

Not until I was taught how to learn was I able to learn. Children with learning disorders have to know what they can and cannot do. Once they have this insight they can develop other skills to compensate, like a blind man who develops a keen sense of hearing.

My former Acadia University professor and dear friend, Don Little, said to me, "Bill, forget trying to learn how to write a paper error-free – you never will. Get your ideas down, and hire someone to edit for you." Once I knew it was okay to use an editor for *everything*, I was free! Today, I have over twenty different books in print. Little helped me define my limitations, so I could create my strategies to overcome them.

Very often children with learning challenges spend too many years trying to learn like everyone else. The fact is they can't, and won't learn the same way. They're not dumb; they're just wired differently, and need to learn a different way. The guilt and shame of not being the same kind of learner turns many children off learning altogether. Thank goodness for schools like Landmark East in Boston and Wolfville, Nova Scotia, founded by William Drake, a man who had a learning disability himself. There are many new private schools appearing, and the public schools are slowly learning how to help affected children, and even adults, in adult day-schools. It's never too late to learn!

What these issues have taught us is that learning isn't only cognitive. It is also important that children and adults grow emotionally as well. Daniel Goleman, author of the *New York Times* best seller, *Emotional Intelligence*, has shown that emotional awareness is as important as traditional intelligence in predicting the future success of an individual. Howard Gardner, author of *Multi Intelligences,* has identified seven important modes of learning: linguistic, logical, bodily-kinesthetic, spatial, musical, interpersonal, intrapersonal and environmental. He advances the theory that each individual has a preferred mode. This again illustrates that there is more than just one area of importance in the development of human intelligence.

If a child spends twelve years reinforcing the idea that learning is pain, it may be a challenge for them to want to learn as they get older. I can tell you from my own experience of failing Grade 2 that school was a struggle. There were other painful memories; so many that I can only really remember three teachers out of my thirteen years in public school – my favourite was my Grade 5 teacher, Ellen Stewart.

It was not until I was 22 that I really learned how to learn. The joy in that revelation has stayed with me to this day. I am in school again, pursuing an MBA, and a Masters in clinical psychology, not because I need it, but because I love it.

There are three things in life that are guaranteed – death and taxes are the first two, as everybody knows, but the third? Ironically, the third certainty is that we will never know enough! We don't stop learning while our heart is beating.

Learning, the path to the future we want, can occur in so many ways: through a formal education, reading, going to church, relationships. The goal of learning is to obtain knowledge. Ideally, it should be the kind of knowledge that helps us without hurting others.

But there tends to be two basic ways in which we apply our knowledge: to make things better, and to make people better. Let's compare the two. What has improved faster in the last century? Our technology or our manners? Our rocket science and weapons systems or peaceful conflict resolution? It is an interesting question, and not as black and white as you may think, but there have been many occasions when we have put technology ahead of civility.

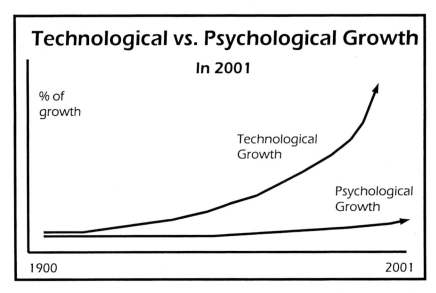

Technological Versus Psychological Growth – adapted from Glasser (1996)

Why have we made the race for advancement more important, it appears, than peace on earth? Because it is easier to be working on something than someone. People are complex, and each one is different. That said, we do need to continue to grow technologically because of the tremendous positive impact it can have on our quality of life. If it were not for the expansive growth in medical science, for example, Sparkle Kitty would not be here today.

My concern is, with so much focus on the machinery of improvement, when do we actually start working on our civility? What message are we ignoring as the rates of drug-related and violent crime increase? What about the fact we still have many children dying of hunger? We can't continue to postpone what is right – after all, the present is the only time we can be sure of having.

When we make our own decision to grow, here and now, we are not only choosing for our individual sake, but for the sake of all. And yet, the world can only improve one person at a time. We may not be able to change *other people,* but that doesn't matter, because we change the *whole* simply by changing what is within our grasp to change – our *part.*

Whether you deny it, have yet to realize it, or practice it in awareness, each one of us has been charged to make this world a better one than we found it. Changing the world may feel like an insurmountable order if you approach the task with your cognitive faculties alone. But you don't have to move mountains to accomplish world change: by changing a small part of the world, i.e. *yourself*, you change the whole. So change your mind, and change your heart, too – your intentions. What is in your heart is in the world.

Again speaking as an educator, I believe we are all on a journey of continual learning and growth. Knowledge propels us because it is power. Here in the first year of a new century, half of the jobs that will be needed in the next seven years *have not even been invented yet*. Some of us may not have to change careers, but most of us will, *if we want to eat!* This doesn't come as a terrible shock to some of us, because for the last twenty years or so, people have changed careers at an unprecedented rate.

Whether you are a fast-paced job-swapper or have pushed the same broom for a significant portion of your life, I invite you to take a few moments to consider the importance of learning in your life:

1. Do you believe the world is changing faster than you are?
2. Do you like to learn?
3. Does the phrase "lifelong learning" inspire you – or break you out in a sweat?
4. Did you know that fewer than 15 percent of adults read books on a regular basis?
5. Do you have a self-study learning plan for personal growth?
6. Do you stay current in your field?
7. Are dramatic changes afoot in your field?
8. If so, how does this affect your job?
9. Are you involved in your children's learning?
10. Do you take courses because you are required to, or because you are interested?

Aside from all the intrinsic benefits, learning does give us marketable expertise. So learning can be justified from many standpoints. If you are required to take courses professionally, the skills you master in the workplace are ones you can use at home too, especially communication and conflict resolution skills.

Jack Walsh, the former chief executive officer of General Electric, developed a university exclusively for GE employees, in order to help them develop personally as well as professionally.

Ken Blanchard, who wrote the best-selling *One-Minute Manager,* also promotes the importance of developing employees' knowledge bases. Both believe the people skills are useful at *work and home.* Helping the employee increases employee retention, customer service and profitability.

On the other end of the continuum, there are more students applying to and attending graduate schools today, partly because an unstable work environment undermines their career choices. It may look impressive statistically to see the climb in attendance, but this is countered by a steady population of students still not finishing high school. We have more individuals entering the upper echelons of academe, while others are not finishing Grade 12 – too many for an advanced industrial society.

As result, literacy is still a problem in North America. According to the Council for Canadian Unity, slightly over 40 percent of Canadian adults do not have the literacy skills necessary to cope adequately with the complexities of modern life. (www.ccu-cuc.ca/)

Beyond the problems of adult illiteracy, the fact is, children are getting smarter earlier in the area of cognitive development, and are maturing later in the area of emotional development.

It appears to me that adolescence is starting around age seven now, and is ending somewhere around twenty-seven, due, in large part, to the under-focus of society on character-building and morals. The debate of whose job "morals" is continues. Teachers say parents need to do more, and parents say teachers need to do more. Unfortunately, teachers are the constant, when parents aren't. I worked with violent youth in a correctional centre for seven years, and these kids all shared a measure of academic failure. I'm not blaming the teachers, but there is research which shows 60 percent of North American prison populations have attention deficit difficulties.

Perhaps one of the problems in our society is a large section of the population did not have the opportunity to learn how to learn, and so lost interest in learning. If you aren't interested in learning your ABCs, it's going to be even harder to interest you in morals.

It does not take an expert in career advancement to demonstrate that learning and the ability to learn, both in a group and individually, are important skills. However, many of the most progressive people in our society achieved their prominence thanks to what they learned on their own.

You may associate Tony Robbins with shiny teeth and infomercials, but the now-famous motivational speaker was, in his own words, a fat, lazy, unhappy man, who lived in a small apartment on his own, feeling down and out, until one day he made the choice to change his world. He started reading, and by the time he had digested his first 700 books, he was well on his way to self-made manhood. The books were in the self-help and improvement vein: Stephen Covey's *The Seven Habits of Highly Effective People* and Napoleon Hill's *Think and Grow Rich,* among others.

We've all heard school boards throw around catch-phrases like "life-long learning" to describe everything from curriculum to renting school space for extra cash. The idea of gradual, orderly, continuous improvement, without capital expenditure, summed up in the Japanese "kaizen" concept, applies equally well to the classroom, the boardroom, or at home.

For a quality life we need to learn both academically and emotionally, and remember that quality is a moving target. If we don't learn, we will fall behind, and fail to obtain what we really want, both personally and professionally. *Learning is fundamental to a quality life!* A few important learning traits are:

1. **Curiosity** – wanting to know, just to know,
2. **Expanding Interests** – wanting more detail ("vertical" knowledge) about more areas ("horizontal" knowledge).
3. **Depth of Interest** – wanting more detail or specialized information about what you like.
4. **Methodicalness** – a systematic arrangement of what you know and what you want to know next.

Because a large number of us get caught up in the routine of life we become victims of money and debt. We end up with a job we hate in a routine we barely have the strength to follow. When asked why we persevere so hard-headedly, what do many of us say? "I have no choice. I am in debt, and I must work." The truth is, if there is *will* there is a *way*. We need to want to learn, so we can get the jobs we want to have, and lead the life we want to live. Jobs only provide a choice of lifestyle – we supply the joy. Doing what you want for a career is really only a part of happiness. However, for many it is everything.

How quickly does a child learn? They learn fast because they find learning fun. For us to learn we need to find a way to attach value to it so we can enjoy the process. We are learning as educators that people learn more in school when it involves *elaborate learning*. This is when there is emotion attached to the learning. This will greatly increase the transfer and retention of new information.

Elaborate learning works on the following premise. You go to a party and have a wonderful time – so wonderful that you have total recall of everything that happened, to this day. Now, the party was thirty years ago. How do you continue to remember it so well? Your emotional system was involved, and it stored all the details in something like your computer's picture file format. When you access this file, it opens up the way your computer's does, and all the emotion that was attached to the original experience provides the clarity and detail. What happens when children enjoy school? They will do what I did in Grade 5 with Ms. Stewart! Learn! Grow!

Human beings are really emotionally driven animals. We rely on our emotions to gauge our well being at any particular moment. Brain research tells us that our emotional states correspond to chemical changes in our brains. Research has incidentally identified "learning drugs" naturally present in the brain. You don't need to know the biochemical formulas to know that when *fun* and *entertainment* are involved, we learn more effectively and efficiently.

State dependent learning can have its drawbacks, however. If we learn something at one level of emotion, but are unable to use it in another emotional state, we haven't fully incorporated the new skill. For example, most people are relatively calm while attending a stress management workshop. When life hits, the same people have not practiced using the skills in an aroused state, thus they mistakenly perceive the skills are of no value. This is why some people say stress workshops wear off. The fact is, they don't wear off the person who practiced what they learned over a period of time, and incorporated the skills for use in *any state*.

How do you define the learning process? Learning is a childmind essential. We need it, not just to stay current in this changing world, but to be good, happy creatures. The way to add learning to your daily experience is to add fun and value to what you do. For me, learning is

**L**ifelong,
**E**motionally involving,
**A**sking questions,
**R**eading,
**N**oticing the world around you,
**I**nterest-based and
**N**on-linear OR
**G**oal-oriented with beginning, middle and ending clearly determined.

Learning helps us define what we know. At some point, we will need to acknowledge the fact that we don't know everything. It isn't wise to pretend to know what we don't. Sometimes we can change this situation by learning more, but sometimes the answer we desire isn't accessible.

Do we have the right to our opinions? Certainly, and as the famous lawyer Gerry Spence said, we have the right to defend them, too. It would be hard to find any lawyer who didn't believe it was healthy to disagree and debate a different point of view, but to do this effectively we need *facts*.

The best way to give an argument legs is to provide the evidence and facts to back it up. As students of life, we gather factual information we can use to form intelligent opinions. The power of learning helps us develop the confidence to state our views.

But sometimes admitting we don't know, when we really don't, is the best favour we can do ourselves (and others). There is no question that learning is fundamental to our well being, but knowledge alone is not enough.

There is nothing more frustrating as an educator than watching people who know better *not do*.

Each person has something called a morphogenetic field, which is an imaginary line we draw at the limit of what we think we are capable of doing. It was once thought that no human being could run a mile in less than four minutes. From commentators to physiologists, no one believed a human body could handle it. But a young Oxford medical student, Roger Bannister, was undeterred from his goal to be the first to break the barrier.

On March 6, 1954, Bannister ran the "Miracle Mile" in 3:59.4. His record lasted only forty-six days, but he can be credited with inspiring even those who beat him.

Many of us set four-minute mile limits in our lives. We learn to settle for second best because we think life is going to be the way it is, and we talk ourselves out of there even being a next level. But there are infinite levels, and getting to the next one is a matter of acquiring the knowledge and *putting it to work*. To get to the next level we need to stretch ourselves. The stretching may hurt. It may require sacrifices. But if you are willing to stretch, you will get results.

It is very common for all new learning to have an up front uncomfortable part. With diligence and time you will grow through these uncomfortable zones. Take public speaking, for example. It may take time to feel comfortable in front of an audience. However, with practice, time, and diligence you will grow and get through this uncomfortable zone. We all need to continuously challenge ourselves to stretch to our fullest potential.

It helps to be aware of the learning curve – many people quit early because they don't make allowances for it. We need to route a behaviour 600 to 700 times before it becomes an automatic habit. So don't get discouraged. All learning goes through these four stages:

**Unconscious Incompetence** – Not knowing that you don't know. Take a toddler who doesn't realize their shoelaces are undone – it may not have occurred to them that they even have shoelaces until they trip them up.

**Conscious Incompetence** – Knowing you do not know. The two-year-old is trying to tie the laces, and crying, because they won't tie themselves.

**Conscious Competence** – Knowing you have the knowledge. Once the two-year-old has been shown how, they discover they can do it if they concentrate.

**Unconscious Competence** – Not even having to think about it. The three- or four-year-old ties their laces with ease.

Even with shoelaces, there is a great deal of relapse between stages two and three. In my research, it takes, on average, 12 to 18 months for a new habit to become ingrained.

In today's world, we need to have many skills – academic and emotional. We need to develop our skills horizontally. We'll do better to accept the fact we can't really train for a job anymore. We need to obtain skills we can adapt to career opportunities as they arise.

**Help Is Available**

Professional Life Coaching is an excellent way for you to get one-on-one teaching to expand your knowledge base. The goal is to get people to their next level, and break through perceived blocks. Some of you may want to keep what you have, and ensure you do not slip. Coaching, based on the mentoring model, will help you stay focused, and on the right track. This particular kind of coaching is not therapy, and is not helpful for people who are mentally ill, mainly because it is a proactive model, not a reparative one. (For more information on coaching please see my web page: www.howattcompany.com.)

**Tips to Improve your Life Learning**

1. If you aren't reading now, start reading. Try it – you'll be amazed. If you read 10 pages a day (most books are fewer than 300 pages), that's a book a month, 12 books a year. How many are you reading now? Reading is a wonderful pastime, and a great way to expand your knowledge base. The time to read, for pleasure and personal growth, is one of the greatest gifts you can give yourself.

2. Take a course for fun, like gardening. There are many offerings at your local community college. Find an area of interest, and get involved.

3. Teach others. One of the best ways to learn is to teach others. Become a volunteer or teaching leader.

4. Watch educational television. Instead of plugging in to your regular cop show, give the Discovery Channel a shot. This will help expand your horizons.

5. Be a role model. If you like learning, promote it with passion, and help people see that you enjoy what you are doing. When children are doing homework, I suggest you turn the TV off, and do your own studying. Send the message you want your children and others to see.

6. Learn a new word each day. Dust off your dictionary, and keep it within reach, or jump on the web and take a tour!

7. Go back and take another degree because you want to – if you can afford it.

8. Listen to taped books while driving.

9. Journal daily to track your life and improve your writing skills. Writing is a great way to improve your ability to express yourself, and to develop your communications skills. It is also a great way for you to put your day into context.

10. Take a humour workshop, and look at how you can add humour and fun to your daily learning. When we can laugh, we can learn. If you aren't laughing enough, explore humour! You'll be adding learning to your life, too!

*In closing . . .*

We'll never know everything, but learning is integral to our emotional well being. Furthermore, in our present age, the world is changing at such a rate that learning has never been more important to our survival. And collectively, learning is the only way we will change our society for the better. Taking time to enjoy learning is part of our calling as human beings, and if we can stay in a learning mindset, it will serve us lifelong.

> Sparkle Kitty Coaching:
> I need to learn, if I am going to fix hearts one day. Learning takes time, but that's OK.

6   THE POWER OF LEARNING

# Sparkle Action

The activities listed below will help you study this chapter, and obtain the learning from it. The way to enhance your knowledge is by studying and self-reflection, and then practice.

1. On a scale of 1 (low) and 10 (high), how much are you already living this childmind principle today? _____

2. List three points from this chapter that may have had special significance for you:

   a) _____

   b) _____

   c) _____

3. How will this principle help you in each of the five *life balance* areas?
   In the space provided, be specific about each area:

   Health: _____

   Self: _____

   Relationships: _____

   Career: _____

   Money: _____

4. What is one area you need to act on?

   _____

   What is your action plan?

   _____

   _____

   _____

   (When you make an action plan I suggest that you break it into small steps. To make any change we need to start out slow and be committed to the process and not the outcome.)

Section 3: The Power of Open Soul

# Chapter 7

# The Power of Faith

*"I am thankful for God!" – Sparkle Kitty*

SPARKLE KITTY picked up the concept of faith fast. At the age of three, when the family was gathered for our Thanksgiving meal, we went around the table, each of us giving thanks for what we were most grateful. I opened with, "I am thankful for my family," then Sherrie added, "I am thankful for my children," and my father and mother each expressed their gratitude for health. When it was Emily's turn, she offered, "I am thankful for God." To hear this was a profound experience for my wife and me. It is important for us to be reminded of the impact faith can have, at any age.

As we start this new millennium, it's clear we have gone through an industrial revolution, a technical revolution, and are now in a spiritual revolution. I am seeing more people than ever before in my thirty-six years asking "why?"

The three big questions that philosophy sets out to answer are:

Who am I? Where did I come from? Where am I going?

Have you ever asked these questions? Have you ever answered them? Have your answers satisfied you? Have your answers changed?

Are you aware of your faith? Do you have one? Whether it is a traditional faith or a faith recognized by organized religion is not the question. Rather, do you have a faith that works for you? Could you do more in this department? Have you thought about doing more and put it off?

We all need to have something to believe in, for gratitude in good times, and solace in hard times. In fact, if you consider a relationship to God – however you perceive

God – as part of your relationship needs, it's quite safe to say that faith not only falls into the life balance equation, but is also a basic human need.

Ultimately, we all have choice, but a spiritual base within and beyond the self promotes healthy choice. Faith helps people establish strong morals, and if it is real faith, it helps people overcome fear and anxiety.

If we make it our common goal to develop more civility in our society, then we must also make faith and spirituality our goal.

In my family, we practice Christianity. My wife and I have chosen to be Christians. From this faith we derive some very important foundations. We are not extreme, in any sense, in our beliefs or practices.

For me, prayer has been an important tool in developing faith.

The day that I learned about prayer was interesting; I was a student at Acadia University, in my second year, and not doing that well academically. My Grade Point Average was 1.35 – I needed help and guidance.

I was walking by the university chapel, and I heard a voice in my mind distinctly say, "Come in."

"For what?" I wondered. The Manning Memorial Chapel is a small, but very beautiful brick building with white Greek columns outside, a white interior, a giant pipe organ, and full-length stained glass windows that are outlined in gold, so they reflect the interior light of the church after the light fades outside.

"I have a deal for you, are you interested?" the voice continued.

"Okay, what?" I thought, remaining open-minded, non-judgemental, and in the moment.

"If you come in and pray for ten minutes daily, you will pass this year and increase your marks," the voice replied. So I did pray, and got my marks up to a B, and passed all my courses.

I was married in this chapel, and to this day, I consider acceptance of that invitation to pray the initial step of my spiritual journey. Although I was down, I was willing to listen and trust my faith. I did not even know I had one, until that day I walked by the church. Now I see prayer as a way to:

# 7 THE POWER OF FAITH

**P**raise all the good in our lives,

**R**elease mistakes, and commit to improvement,

**A**sk for forgiveness,

**Y**earn for guidance,

**E**nter a peaceful state of mind through which insight and self-knowledge are possible,

**R**equest help for others, as well as ourselves.

When we become aware of the power of prayer, it offers great benefits.

A handful of studies have shown that not all of these benefits appear to be self-induced, contrary to popular belief. Although it has generally been accepted that prayer and meditation can lower blood pressure, and are a practical means of dealing with anxiety and depression, prayer can also help others – even when they aren't aware someone is interceding for them.

A Duke University study in 1998 was among the first.

According to an article in the Greensboro *News & Record*, Baptists and Buddhists alike prayed for strangers in Durham hospital beds:

"Duke University doctors, studying non-traditional influences on healing, lumped about 20 heart patients into a 'prayer group.' The patients didn't know it, but their names were listed on prayer requests sent to places like Nepal, Jerusalem and Baltimore, where people of different faiths prayed for their recovery.

Those prayers worked, doctors say. Patients in the "prayer group" performed 50 to 100 percent better than patients who weren't the prayer targets.

Results of the study -- and others from around the country -- are jolting the traditional medical establishment, where prayer has long been tagged a medical taboo."

The study, of course, has touched off a great controversy. The only thing the medical establishment has agreed upon is that more study of the phenomenon is required. A similar study, undertaken at St. Luke's Hospital in Kansas City, Missouri, was detailed in the *Archives of Internal Medicine* in 1999. Again, patients were prayed for without their knowledge.

In Kansas, almost a thousand heart patients were divided into two groups. The first group was prayed for daily by volunteers for four weeks. The second group was not. The volunteers who prayed for "a speedy recovery with no complications" did not know the patients – they only knew their first names. The result: after four weeks, the prayed-for patients experienced about 10 percent fewer complications, which were defined as ranging from chest pain to cardiac arrest.

There are many different ways to pray and meditate – sitting, kneeling, lying down. But the important part of maintaining a certain posture, or doing it in a certain place, or at a specific time, is to be aware that you are doing it, so that your thoughts don't wander off into undisciplined rambling – although praying, after all, has less to do with "thinking" than feeling. Intercessory prayer is a way of sending love to others.

Meditation specifically aims to clear the mind, and calm the surface waves of "ego," so the heart, the true depths of the inner self, can be known. But there are different forms of meditation, and themes on which to meditate. Metta meditation, in particular, is very similar to prayer. "Metta" is the Pali word for loving-kindness, or compassion. The metta practitioner sends their love out to people in ever-widening circles, to ultimately include the people who challenge them, as well as the people close to them.

I see meditation as an excellent tool to help yourself achieve a sense of peace and balance. There are many books on how to meditate – which one you read isn't as important as learning how, and doing it. Prayer and meditation will improve your life!

**Why Have Faith?**

You don't need to believe in a white-bearded guy on a throne to pray. In fact, that sort of idea may even get in the way. But in addition to praying for all the practical reasons, it is my personal belief that faith is the underlying relationship we have with God, through our souls, for all time – and beyond time.

I define soul as our "God-connection," a sort of spiritual umbilical, if you will. You may not be able to perceive it that way with your senses, but with time and practice, you will see evidence of it working in your life, if you let it.

For me, spiritual guidance has an unmistakable feel to it. When I am on purpose, and I see my intentions with clarity, my mind, body, and spirit are in balance. I feel a sense of oneness with the universe. Over time, this has allowed me to identify and release many of the character flaws that held me back – responses so habitual they occupied "blind spots" in my awareness. I continually overlooked them.

Unfortunately, many people may live their entire lives in those blind spots. Our society has gone off course big time. Too many of us are motivated by stuff and money. Morals are not a high priority. Since the passing of the Victorian era, we have made morals disposable. Indeed, to be concerned about morals today is to be considered by some Victorian, puritanical, emotional, or even stupid. It's considered quaint, in some circles, to have scruples.

We rely on the law for the last word, when the law is really the minimal standard society will accept, the lowest common denominator, as it were. (Perhaps this is because the law can only impose restrictions on our outward behaviour – not our inward behaviours, thoughts, feelings, beliefs. And we need to change from the inside out.)

George Bernard Shaw, the great dramatist and iconoclast, said we live this life so that we can get in touch with our existence. As a society, we are out of touch. According to the Thomas Jefferson Research Institute, morals constituted 90 percent of all teaching in the 1770s, less than six percent in 1926, and by 1951 it was so low it could not be measured.

Wisdom is based on self-knowledge, the discovery of that which we are. Morals are the warp on which the fabric of character is woven. But there would be no fabric – no threads – without you finding a meaning for your life. Faith is often the means or result of a search for meaning.

Never has it been so important to define who we are to get to where we want to be. Learning who we are, a question many of us struggle with daily, is a part of the huge challenge of civility. Until we can define life for ourselves, it is impossible to do it for others. We have a great void of emotional loss in our society. We have too many people who are lost. Before others can find you, you must find yourself. The quest for spirituality is one way to increase your chances of finding yourself. I believe in GOD; you have the choice to or not to. For me, GOD does the following:

**G**uides me; I need only ask for direction and it will be offered.

**O**bserves my intentions.

**D**etermines limits to the extent that I can only do my best.

While I am always free to choose my state of mind, I may also be faced with circumstances I did not consciously choose.

You will, in the end, need to define what you believe in and what G.O.D. stands for in your books. Once this was clear in my mind, I was able to do develop my spirituality. My faith expanded. My soul unfolded.

I believe that in this new time, more of us are starting to look inward, searching for our faith. I believe that more of us are wondering who we really are and what we are supposed to do on earth. Are you searching for your faith? For me, faith means:

**F**orgiving yourself and others.

**A**ligning your actions with your intentions.

**I**ntending with clarity and awareness – through individual prayer or meditation.

**T**eaching, by example, the principles that are wise and true for all human

**H**ouse which we can enter at any time. A haven, a refuge.

Many moving parts make a world of change. Technology is accelerating, but as people we are falling behind. In the midst of change, a solid faith is a great foundation. It is peace of mind to know we have a consistent guide, a compass when we are in unfamiliar territory.

All faith is based on a spiritual awareness that leads to a spiritual awakening. We all make this journey a little differently – yet the many paths are one. From my experience, asking yourself questions, and searching for your own answers is where it starts. I suggest you explore the following questions:

1. How do you now define spirituality in your life?
2. Do you see the value of adding faith to your life?
3. Are you prepared to explore faith in your life?
4. If you have not made a faith inquiry, what has stopped you?
5. What would need to happen for you to begin?
6. Are you wondering why you are here?
7. Have you arrived at a satisfactory answer?
8. Are you at peace with who you are?
9. Have you ever thought about spirit influencing mind? Or mind influencing matter?
10. Do you think faith could be a place to find answers about living?

## Overcoming Character Flaws and Bad Karma

We all are faced with the reality of character flaws. The first step in overcoming these limitations is to stop denying they exist – or blaming others for them! Taking ownership of one's shortcomings and mistakes is a major step in the direction of self-responsibility. The consistent application of awareness is the rest of the job.

I believe we need to do a certain amount of work to enjoy happiness and peace. If I pay my power bill I deserve to have power. If I don't, I shouldn't be surprised if my power is cut. If I work hard and help others, I deserve to have good things happen to me. Every action returns to me in kind – or unkind! This is what is also known as the law of karma. It's the corollary of the golden rule. Do unto others as you would have them do unto you; for what you do unto others will be done to you. We are all sowers and reapers.

Nevertheless, there are times when bad things happen to good people, when innocent people are the victims of others' crimes. Some religions address this problem by talking about karma over many lifetimes, about justice being administered in an afterlife. But if we are living in the here and now, we have to accept that there are certain limits that go along with being human, and that every moment we are given is a gift. (A "present.")

Unfortunately, most people associate "deserving" with the realm of material work and material reward; but to deserve anything good in life, material or otherwise, I believe we need to live with high personal morals, and have a clear and honourable intent, or in other words:

**D**o what is necessary with commitment and compassion,
**E**arn credibility with yourself and others,
**S**tay on your path and work to eliminate character flaws,
**E**ducate yourself at every opportunity,
**R**ealign yourself when you get off course,
**V**alue what you've been given,
**E**valuate the impact of your actions on yourself and others.

When we are able to act accordingly, we *deserve* to live life in a manner that is more likely to help bring us success in many ways, not just materially. To have a healthy soul, or an open connection with God, we need character strength.

There are many questions that are left unanswered in this world. When we start to explore who we can be right now, we are able to grasp what we have come from, and where we are going. From observing Sparkle Kitty, I can see the benefit of continuing to grow in my faith as I grow as a human being. In fact, it has only been in the last few years that I have truly begun exploring my faith and spirituality. This new journey has led me to more peace of mind, particularly in those times when I am looking for direction. I have more work ahead of me, but I once heard that a good first step is half of your success.

**Ten Tips to Add Faith to Your Life**

1. Be willing to listen to learn about faith. You need to ask questions, but listen to the answers. I suggest you ask questions about yourself first, and then move on to your friends and family.
2. Faith does not have to be traditional. The search for spirituality is a personal adventure. There is no set path. All you need to do is start – the path will be made for you.
3. Don't rule out the traditional. Pick a church, and give the tried and true a shot. You may be very surprised by what you'll learn. (Vietnamese Zen Buddhist Thich Nhat Hanh advises people to return to their root tradition, and make peace with it: "Many years ago, I recognized that by understanding your own tradition better you also develop increased respect, consideration, and understanding for others.")
2. Read a few books on faith and spirituality to provide you with a frame of reference to begin your journey. A good book to start with is the Bible.
3. Set up a meeting with a spiritual counsellor to explore what spirituality and faith are for you.
4. Make a spiritual retreat to explore faith, and experience its influence on your own life.
5. Start to journal your life, and explore themes and questions that you have. Use the journal as a tool to explore who you are and where you are headed.

6. Think about what you want out of spirituality in terms of what you can offer others.
7. Consider the metaphor of a river. Spirituality is like a river flowing all the time. When you are ready to explore, it is always moving and ready to take you on the journey. In other words, you can start anytime and anywhere you want.
8. The power of spirituality in your life cannot be appreciated until you practice. In other words, you won't know until you *start* what it will really do for you. Take the time and explore; it's free and the benefits are priceless.

As you start or continue your spiritual journey, it is important that you understand you are entitled to have your own connection and your own special individual slant on faith – with one quid pro quo (even Aladdin's genie had a few of these) – it cannot be a faith that belittles others' beliefs, or detracts from civility as a whole. Whatever the model or doctrine you employ, the message I want to make clear to you is that *faith*, however you define it, is a wonderful way to enhance your life. It is a great way to access more peace, joy, and serenity in this form as you walk on this planet Earth.

Whether we take on a new belief in God, or let go of an old belief in self, a leap of faith involves the same surrender of rationality and ego. Although faith ultimately involves your entire being, it is through the heart, not the head, that it makes its presence known. For this reason, children, under most circumstances, embrace spirituality without reservation. This is why Jesus was so quick to point out to us that "the kingdom of heaven belongs to little ones such as these."

> *At that time the disciples came to Jesus, saying, "Who then is greatest in the kingdom of heaven?"*
> *Then Jesus called a little child to Him, set him in the midst of them,*
> *And said, "Assuredly, I say to you, unless you are converted and become as little children, you will by no means enter the kingdom of heaven.*
> *"Therefore whoever humbles himself as this little child is the greatest in the kingdom of heaven.*
> *"Whoever receives one little child like this in My name receives Me. (Matthew 18:1-5)*

Although the questioning of adolescence is an inevitable part of the maturing of faith, some of us get waylaid, and never find our way back. Some wish to remain adolescents for life. At so many cross-roads, we roar our engines, and blare our big-name speakers, sound and fury signifying ego. We glance insecurely across the traffic, to see who's looking. We don't want to get old. We don't want to die. We want to be in the driver's seat forever.

Well, if you're at all interested in wisdom, you may have already started to realize that always being in the driver's seat can also be a bit of a chore. And pimples are gross. Look at the little kid, all trussed up in the child-restraint system. Does he care? No, he's looking out the window, with a goofy kind of smile. In between asking, "Are we there yet?" he's counting the cows, the Volkswagens, the burger stands. He's looking up at the shapes of clouds, the colours of leaves, the raindrops hitting the windshield. And just before he reaches over to pinch his sister, there is peace in the car.

*In closing . . .*

We all want to know why we are here. You may frame this question differently, but we all have times when we wonder who we are and what we are really supposed to be doing in this life. Few things are truly free, but the power of spirituality and faith doesn't cost a cent, and it carries one of the biggest pay-offs I have ever known.

Sparkle Kitty Coaching:
God knows everything; we just need to ask.

# Sparkle Action

The activities listed below will help you study this chapter, and obtain the learning from it. The way to enhance your knowledge is by studying and self-reflection, and then practice.

1. On a scale of 1 (low) and 10 (high), how much are you already living this childmind principle today? _____

2. List three points from this chapter that may have had special significance for you:

    a) _____

    b) _____

    c) _____

3. How will this principle help you in each of the five *life balance* areas?
   In the space provided, be specific about each area:

    Health: _____

    Self: _____

    Relationships: _____

    Career: _____

    Money: _____

4. Is there one insight that requires action now?

    _____

    List the steps of your action plan here:

    _____

    _____

    _____

    What is one insight you believe you need to act on?

    _____

# Chapter 8
# The Power of Family and Relationships

*"I love Howatts!" – Sparkle Kitty*

WE were talking about our favourite brand names one day, when Sparkle Kitty said, "I love *Howatts.*"

Brand loyalty was something soda pop manufacturers counted on during the "cola wars" of the 1980s. For Sparkle Kitty, brand loyalty means being committed to her family, and she is very discriminating: "I like everybody else, but they are not Howatts."

Our family is the central sun of her quality world. Perhaps Sparkle Kitty takes family seriously because I do. I consider my family my preferred brand, too. For me, blood is thicker than Coca-Cola!

I consider my family brand permanent, too. Thankfully, we're not in the cattle-breeding business, and no one needs to be stamped with a hot iron. My genetic heritage is recorded in every cell of my body – and my children's. DNA, seen from that point of view, can never be lost, no matter how badly family members get along. And if you do get along, you should take advantage of the wonderful opportunity you have.

My family is a reflection of who I wanted to be when I was a child. I wanted to have a loving father and mother, which I did. I was adopted, and saved from many unknowns. Having my own children has been like seeing water changed into wine. Of all the miracles I have witnessed, they are the ones of which I am the most keenly aware, because when I see them, I see me.

In the play *No Exit,* by French philosopher Jean-Paul Sartre, hell is a place where there are no mirrors. The characters must look into each other's eyes to see themselves.

One of Sartre's most famous lines, "L'enfer c'est les autres," (Hell is others) is the premise of the play. This may be an interesting commentary on the self-centredness of our human condition, which indeed there may be no escaping – but does it have to be hell? I think this is up to us to choose for ourselves, in true existentialist fashion.

According to William Glasser in *Reality Therapy In Action,* just about all human conflict originates in relationships.

Our experience of enjoying life – or not – depends largely on the quality of our relationships. We all need at least one healthy relationship in place to be happy and healthy human beings.

In the second-last scene of the 1996 movie *Jerry Maguire*, Dicky Fox, the mentor of sports agent Jerry Maguire, sums up his own life and point of view: "Hey, I don't have all the answers. In life, to be honest, I've failed as much as I've succeeded. But I love my wife, and I love my life, and I wish you my kind of success."

If, in a lifetime, we are able to maintain functional ties with our own spouse, children, parents and siblings, and two or three close friends, we will have done extremely well.

More relationships than those is wonderful (provided you don't have so many that they all suffer), but fewer isn't always advisable. Even with all the time constraints of life, it is still important to have family *and* friends. Things aren't always smooth in both arenas at the same time, and members of one group can provide counsel as you seek to sort out your issues with members of the other group.

All told, in one lifetime, hundreds, if not thousands, of people come to know us through these relationship gateways:

1. Partner relationships – i.e., spouse.
2. Parenting relationships – with your parents and with your children.
3. Family relationships – i.e., siblings, cousins, in-laws.
4. Life friends, i.e. your best friends in the world; the ones you know that would be there under any circumstance.
5. Acquaintances – the people you have met and know, although you may not stay in continual contact.
6. Work relationships.
7. Organization and club relationships.

All mutually beneficial relationships require time, effort, commitment, loyalty, patience, and a non-judgmental attitude.

Do you have close and solid relationships in your life? Are you happy with them? If not, what are you doing to help them become all you want? In relationships, I often find people are waiting for "the other" to make the change first.

Waiting, in this instance, can cost you precious time. If you have relationships that are not the way you want them, then it is your responsibility to take charge, and do what *you* can to make things better. That means you need to be willing to make changes without expecting the other to change right away. If, in time, things do not improve, then you have a choice.

The power of family and relationships is a theme that Sparkle Kitty has rung loud in my ears. She is so proud to be part of a family; she is sometimes at a loss to put her conviction into words. If you have a loving family, you probably know how that feels!

You don't need a marriage certificate to start a family. There are many different kinds of families, and the paper won't give you the bond, if it's lacking. Love is what you need to start a family. But for me, the word family implies the presence of children.

Having children should go along with a lifelong effort to preserve the relationship that gave them life. You have the right to choose how to accomplish this, but it is important to be aware of the impact of your decisions on others.

I started writing this chapter on the day before Christmas. I was away, but called home. I asked Sparkle Kitty what Christmas meant for her. She said, "Daddy, for it to be a great Christmas you need to be home with us."

Sherrie and I have made family time a high priority in our marriage. We both see the importance of not just quality time, but quantity time *for* true quality. Sparkle Kitty's recognition of the importance of family makes it even harder to ignore! You don't need to have children to develop gratitude for a loving relationship, but it can help.

Family and relationships depend on daily activity and experience. Elaborate functions on special occasions are only a part of the whole equation. Food and gifts are wonderful, but soon forgotten. Putting on an act for the holidays is not enough, especially if the emphasis on presentation distracts us from our daily functioning.

If we are unhappy in our family relationships, we are not functioning as a family. The truth remains that we are a family even if we are miserable. Indefinite misery will wear down our relationships and health.

The increasing divorce rate, and the extremely high failure rate of new business partnerships would seem to suggest that a lot of human beings have difficulty with the long-term sustenance of daily effort any relationship requires.

The ratio of new marriages to divorces in a given year is now 2:1 according to the American Census Bureau. However, the oft-quoted 50 percent failure rate is misleading, as it excludes older marriages, and includes persons who may have married multiple times – therefore it should not be interpreted as 50 percent of people getting divorced! The rise has been apparent since the advent of the no-fault divorce. More accurately, 43 per cent of marriages end within 15 years.

The U.S. Small Business Administration reports that 75 percent of new businesses fail in their first year, and 25 percent of the survivors fail in the second year.

Perhaps we would embrace this effort more willingly if we thought of our contributions in terms of teamwork.

If *team* can be defined as at least two people working for a common goal, all relationships are teams. At a minimum, the goal is the energy that creates the unity of the two. Management training guru Peter Ducker says the same rules apply, regardless of the nature of the team. A band can't make music unless each member plays their own instrument properly. A football team can't even make a play unless each member of the team does his assigned task – the centre gives the ball to the quarterback, the line blocks tackle, and the receiver catches.

In reality, teams are an illusion. What transforms a group of individuals into a team is:

**T**ogether, they have the same goals.

**E**ach member is responsible for their own actions.

**A**ll members have an action to perform, and this way

**M**embership is sharing support and success.

A strong team does not fight over who slipped up. This is not important! What is important is that the team be able to work together for a common purpose. Blame is the single most destructive force for relationships and teams. Judgement creates division.

Too many people lose their love in a relationship because the little things left unresolved build up. What destroys many relationships is the lack of daily focus on the relationship. Sometimes people get so busy they do not make home a priority, and they lose focus on the relationships there. When we do not spend time with a partner or family, we are at great risk of losing what we have. There is no substitute for time. There is no diamond big enough to replace *you*.

The functional family or relationship is a tricky animal to pin down. Why? Because of the variables involved.

Here's the math:

A couple has only one relationship to worry about. One two-way dynamic:

A-B

A couple with one child has a three-way family dynamic, with three two-way relationships:

A-B; A-C; B-C

A couple with two children has a four-way family dynamic, with four three-way relationships:

AB-C; AB-D; A-CD; B-CD

As well as *six* two-way relationships:

A-B; A-C; A-D; B-C; B-D; C-D

Now here's where it starts to get *really* interesting. A family of five has five four-way relationships, *25 three-way relationships, and 10 two-way relationships.* All told, that's *40* relationships, in addition to the basic five-way dynamic.

That means that at any point in time, the family system is working to balance 40 separate inter-relationships. Now add each family member's work relationships, school relationships, and peers. How many hundred relationships is the family working to manage now?

With all of the family and personal relationships we are a part of or party to, there is a great deal of sifting required on our part to achieve a sense of balance. What is the consequence when mother's work is not going well? How does this affect the entire family system? Many times when we are out of tune with one relationship we perceive as a *pillar,* the entire family will feel the effects: "If Mamma ain't happy, ain't *nobody* happy."

Similarly, the entire family will be out of balance if Dad is. This is why people are encouraged "not to take their work home with them." It works the other way too. Indeed, many spouses develop into "workaholics" so they can hide from home.

Are there really any 100 percent functional families? All families will go out of balance by times. The key measurement of interest for me is how long they remain out of balance. A healthy family will work to help each member become balanced, and to weigh out their daily interactions.

Interpersonal skills are a major factor in determining how positively one family member can affect the others. Consider the family of five again; what impact does the age variance have? How does maturity enter the equation? Personality? As you can see, there are many variables at work.

**Relationships Are Challenging – But We Need Them**

The truth is that all human beings need at least one person or animal with whom to relate. We all need relationships – unless we suffer psychopathic deficiencies. Psychopaths lack the ability to trust, empathize, and form affectionate relationships. Psychopathy begins in early childhood – which points to the importance of the nurturing children receive in the first three years of life.

I believe that anyone who reads this book needs a relationship in their life. I believe it is a basic need that we are all driven to fulfil. This is not a matter of choice – we all need a relationship in our lives. Nevertheless, few us know how to keep them, and learn to enjoy them.

**Improving Communication Skills**

I believe that increasing communication skills will assist us in all our relationships. Communication breaks down into these categories:
1. 55% is non-verbal – body language.
2. 35% is preverbal – not what you say but how you say it.
3. 10% is words – what you are actually saying.

When you look at this breakdown, it is clearly important to be as aware of the message as the words themselves. Rapport is built on clear, concise messages.

The meaning of all communication hinges on the way it is received. If there is miscommunication, it is important not to waste time on who was right or wrong. There is no right! Focus instead on clarity and accuracy. Always consider the alternate meanings a message can hold, but focus on the positive ones. From my research, I can say that ninety-nine percent of all relationship problems grow out of miscommunication. It is of great importance to learn how to build rapport with each other so you can reduce the number of miscommunications.

**Techniques for Building Rapport**

The purpose of these techniques is to help you build trust with another individual when you are conversing. When you communicate effectively, you will expand the comfort zone of your interactions together, and the relationship will develop more easily. Learning and practicing the techniques listed below will help you decrease miscommunication – the agent and origin for most conflict:

1. *Conversation speed* – If someone talks slowly, match their speed. If they talk fast, talk fast. Be aware of the speed of the conversation.
2. *Integrate favourite words* – In conversation, listen to the person's language and favourite words. Use these words in your conversation.
3. *Similar body language* – observe the person's body language. For example, are their legs crossed? If so, mirror them as closely as you can. It is not important that you are exactly the same. You want to avoid leaning back in your chair if they lean back. Stay in the "e" position, leaning slightly toward them, to appear interested. The trick to mirroring body language is to act as though they are pacing you. You do not need get entirely caught up in imitating them; just be as similar as you can without being obvious.
4. *Voice volume* – match their voice volume as closely as you can.
5. *Proxemics* – Be aware of their personal space. Watch for non-verbal cues, and do not violate their personal boundaries.
6. *Observe Favourite Predicts* – If a person is visual, they will talk fast, use large hand gestures and predicting words like "see, look, and watch." If a person is auditory, they will talk with a voice speed that is slower than visual; will be very aware of their pronunciation of words; will have body gestures around the middle of their body; and use predicts like "hear, listen, and talk." If a person is kinaesthetic they will talk more deeply and slowly, and have few body gestures,

because they are focusing on sensations. They will use predicts like "feel, grasp, and touch." Once you observe the person's favourite communication style, you can really increase rapport by matching their model of communication and using their predicts.

7. *Stop and Hear Me* – conversation is an art. It is important to learn when to talk, and when to listen. When in doubt, listen, and be interested in what others have to say.
8. *Ask Questions* – instead of talking endlessly about yourself, ask others interesting questions about who they are. Don't worry about sounding nosy! Most people are flattered by attention, and love the opportunity to talk about themselves.
9. *Let a person stop on their own* – it is important not to cut others off or interrupt. Finish listening to what others have to say before preparing your next comment.
10. *Have a model to get out of conflict* – have a plan for resolving conflict. Design the plan yourself, or read up on conflict resolution.

These ten techniques will help you build rapport with others. They will take practice! I suggest you master one skill at a time. Once you have all ten skills in hand, you will have a great technical base on which to build relationships.

For a relationship to work, it needs to make sense, and partners need to live up to each other's needs by being:

**R**ealistic – remember, people won't change unless they want to.
**E**thical – earning each other's trust, being honest with each other.
**L**oyal to each other, and not swayed by temptation.
**A**lert to each other's changing needs and natures. This requires listening.
**T**olerant of each other's mistakes and patient while working to rectify them
**I**nvolved in each other's interests.
**V**ocal! Vibrant debate is necessary sometimes.
**E**nergetic – investing new energy on a daily basis.

These are some of the traits needed for a relationship to grow and stay strong. All healthy relationships are very rewarding, and the price we pay to keep them is never too much, unless other relationships or our own health are affected.

Since Sparkle Kitty came along, I have come to take my commitment to family very seriously. It's an unconditional commitment; it's lifelong; and it's every day. I yearn to be with my family as much as I can. This time is the fuel that helps me get through each day, and the motivation for a great deal of what I do. As a father, I am highly motivated and committed to do what is needed to provide for my family. I also want to ensure that I have time with my family so I can continually remind myself of why I am working hard.

In a society that is continuously changing, many people want to keep up with what is new. Many people would rather replace and dispose of things than fix them, and that goes for relationships as well. I see too many giving up on their relationships for frivolous reasons. Separation shouldn't be considered first unless there are issues like abuse, addictions, or cults – then the children, particularly, should be in a place where they are *safe*.

However, too many couples fall out of love with each other, and do not do the work to fall in love again. Children are the victims of these wars. In my time spent working with young offenders, I have seen many children who were making top grades before their parents separated. The loss of one's family has such an impact and causes such grief that many adolescents, in particular, end up compensating for the loss with crime and drugs. It sounds extreme, but it's a reality for many young people.

Divorce in the twenty-first century is creating a great deal of unnecessary pain. People who get married need to be responsible and take this commitment more seriously. We need to ensure we are compatible, and take training if we do not know how to assess this. We need to keep ourselves balanced so we can manage life and love. We cannot give up and throw away our dreams! We need to take a stance to value and honour the family unit! People change, and we need to work to change together. Make it as though there is no other option! We need to work hard, and make sure we build a strong family unit. This is what we are all here for – to serve each other, especially our families. This is part of the reason human beings have such a long lifespan compared to other members of the creature world. We are not only driven to reproduce, but to protect and guide our offspring as well. To do this, we need to stick around!

Good parenting is a very important element of helping our children become good parents themselves. Because parenting skills aren't taught in schools, most of our parenting skills come directly from what we were taught by our parents when they raised us (which may be far short of ideal). So, often for better or worse, we role model and use what we were taught. But the world is changing, and how we parent may need to change as well. Differing parenting philosophies are sometimes a reason couples split up. To help you parent better, I suggest you review the following ten points:

1. Learn your child's personality type. All children are special. Get to learn what makes your child tick, and how to manage them. If you don't know how, ask for help.

2. Learn how to use verbal interventions – to ask questions and avoid statements. When you want a child to do something, try using ALDR. This stands for
**A**sk the child to do what you want them to do.
**L**isten to what they have to say, and hear them. Learn their point of view.
**D**istract them with a future opportunity to do something with you once your request is done.
**R**edirect them with a direct request. Only say the request, nothing else – repeat the statement until you have compliance.

3. *NEVER HIT – NEVER, EVER! NO EXCUSES!* All hitting does is teach that aggression is a way to get what you want. There is always a better way. Never bribe – all this teaches the child is that to do something they need to get something. What do you do, then? Role model, and teach self-responsibility.

4. Slow down, and spend lots of time with your children – be interested in their world.

5. Be a role model, and practice what you preach. Ensure you both are on the same page, and always be firm, fair, and consistent. Children like structure and routine.

6. Be kind to your partner, and show them love.

7. Play with your children, and enjoy it.

8. Read to your children.

9. Model the nine childmind principles to your children.

10. Take parent and relationship training. This is invaluable. Many of us have never taken any training. We rely on what we know, and hope this is going to be enough.

My children help to define me, and as a father, I believe it is my job to help define them. My actions will determine a great deal – so, if my children are angry at times, I have to look to my own behaviour. Very rarely are children born bad. They can be born broken, but never bad.

For all families and relationships, you need to start with a common frame of reference, so each member of the family knows what is expected of them. We must all be aware of our partner's and children's wants and needs, without neglecting our own. We need to take care of ourselves first to be able to take care of others. The following tips should help with the process:

**Ten Tips for Building Your Family and Relationships**

1. Treat people the way *they* want to be treated – not necessarily the way *you* would. Make it the family rule. The golden rule, after all, is a rule of thumb, and it does have limitations. If your daughter doesn't want to be seen with you at the mall, try to think of it in teen-age terms, not adult terms. George Bernard Shaw spoke truly, albeit cynically, when he said: "Do not do unto others as you would that they should do unto you. Their tastes may not be the same."

2. Monitor the following: Doing *at*, *for* and *with*. If you are doing *at*, you are usually talking *a lot* – correcting, criticizing and directing; doing *for*, you are prompting, driving, remembering, buying, and giving people homework answers; but when you are doing *with*, you are spending time. Ensure you are doing more *with* than anything else.

3. In your relationships ensure you clearly define what your roles are – do not make assumptions. Put them in writing, and define what your jobs are – and are not – in the relationship.

4. Establish clear boundaries in writing about what the rules are and the consequences for the breach of agreements.

5. Define in writing a family purpose and values. What are the main goals of the family?
6. Remove coercion and punishment – they do not work. They may get quick results for the short term, and create wedges for the future. Motivate people by helping them see the intrinsic rewards of accomplishment.
7. If you need help in an area, *get it*. Some problems just don't fix themselves. Too many leave what they know is broken to hope. There are coaches and workshops out there to help you. *Ask!*
8. You will cannot change the will of others. Forget it! All you can do is build rapport, and negotiate the relationship.
9. Be as firm, fair, and consistent as possible. These three checks will keep your actions in balance.
10. It takes two to have a relationship. Just because you are parents does not mean you will automatically have a relationship. Relationships are earned – they are fifty-fifty deals that require the participation of both parties. (Review *A Relationship Survival Guide for the 21st Century* and *A Parent's Survival Guide for the 21st Century* for help with both.)

All relationships take work, effort, and commitment. I find it amazing how my Sparkle Kitty knows this. If we forget things that are this basic, as we get older, what else can we learn from our children? They do not consider family life optional. They only see we need to work everything out and be together. This is wisdom that can be applied to other aspects of life: *anything worth having takes time and effort.* My family is worth anything and everything to me – because it defines me. How about your family or relationship? Would you like it to define who you are? Are you doing all you can to build your relationships? If not, what are you doing?

### *In closing . . .*

We all need to have connections to others. We need relationships if we want to have children, and children become more and more important as we grow older. Many people focus on other things "to get ready" for a loving relationship. Women may miss out on children altogether if they hold out for the perfect career and/or the perfect mate. Older couples may find their health has started to fail.

*Now* is the time to build the bridges and relationships in your world. There is no better time than the present – if you don't believe it, test it. Take an inventory of your present life situation, and ensure you are acting daily to build your relationships. One of the biggest rewards in life is to know you are loved, and know you have people to love. To do this, we need to spend time *with* and time doing.

> **Sparkle Kitty Coaching:**
> Be kind, and everything will be okay.

## Sparkle Action

The activities listed below will help you study this chapter, and obtain the learning from it. The way to enhance your knowledge is by studying and self-reflection, and then practice.

1. On a scale of 1 (low) and 10 (high), how much are you already living this childmind principle today? _____

2. List three points from this chapter that may have had special significance for you:

    a) _____

    b) _____

    c) _____

3. How will this principle help you in each of the five *life balance* areas?
   In the space provided, be specific about each area:

    Health: _____

    Self: _____

    Relationships: _____

    Career: _____

    Money: _____

4. What is one insight you believe you need to act on?
    _____

    What is your action plan?
    _____

    List the steps here:
    _____
    _____
    _____

# Chapter 9
# The Power of Dreams

*"I will fix hearts some day!" – Sparkle Kitty*

FROM the time that Sparkle Kitty knew what a job was – soon after she started talking – she made it clear that she wanted to fix hearts. Her motivation is that when she gets older, she wants to do what Dr. Ross did for her: "fix kids' hearts so they can stay with their parents." Sparkle Kitty understood that the surgery saved her life. She wears her scar today with a great deal of pride.

To share with you how Dr. Ross has helped our family is difficult to express in words. This year, seven years after the operation, our doctors in Halifax told us Emily is doing great, and that Dr. Ross' results were as good as we could get anywhere in the world.

It was a different sort of feeling the time we saw Dr. Ross before the surgery, when we had to sign a release form explaining the risks involved. My wife and I were in shock and disbelief over what would happen to our baby girl. He looked at us, dropped his pen, and said something I will always remember: "Mr. and Mrs. Howatt, I need to tell you, I have done this operation many times, and I know what I need to do. If anything goes wrong, I will be personally devastated."

Only then did my wife and I truly feel he was a part of our team, and with us in the cause 100 percent. Dr. Ross had shown us his commitment to saving our child, which he did! Because of his skill and obvious success in the operation he performed, my wife and I have been able to enjoy watching Emily create her own dreams. What better gift for a parent than to see their child grow? I'm convinced children are truly a gift from God.

What Sparkle Kitty becomes in life in regard to career is not of great importance to me. Her desire to dream is what is important. From dreaming, she will eventually set the path she is going to take that will create her reality.

To obtain our real wants, we must first have a dream. All dreams require us to ask for what we want to have, and this starts with a vision. Once we say what we want, then we have the task to figure out how to do it. When John F. Kennedy told the American Congress in 1961 that he wanted an American to be first to walk on the moon, the technology was not yet present. He created a dream for all Americans. He stated the "what," and left the "how" to the people.

Before you can have a how, you need to need have a complete vision of the dream. It is important to never limit your dreams. Once you create the vision of what you want, then it is of great value to learn to believe you can figure out the how. Although it may take incredible effort and focus, your dreams can really come true.

**The Path of Turning Dreams into Reality**

Step 1. Dreams are your visions of what you see possible. Create a vision of what you want in your life, and be specific.

Step 2. Define your life purpose, based on your beliefs and values. Ensure your dreams are congruent with your values.

Step 3. From your dreams, you must define your role and rules of conduct.

Step 4. The plan of action you take will be the key to learning and discovering the *hows*.

Step 5. Daily evaluation will keep you on course once you have your master plan.

Step 6. Following the nine childmind principles is important for all dreams.

One of the greatest glories we experience in our lives is when our dreams come true. Our dreams help define our purpose. Without action, our dreams remain dreams. Dreams come from our beliefs and values – our sense of who we are, and what we want to accomplish. Our values determine our motivation, which propels our dreams. Sparkle Kitty has reminded me of the power of having dreams. Do you have a dream?

# 9 THE POWER OF DREAMS

Have you ever stopped dreaming? What kills dreams? As we get older, we accumulate so much that our lives can get as out of balance as a neglected cheque book. Our daily routines need maintenance too. Many of us operate in survival mode, e.g., just paying the bills. For many, the pressure of just surviving distracts them so completely that they forget to keep working on their dreams. With so many perceived distractions the majority of these people do not take the time to get back on track. *Why?* They get caught up in life's routines and potholes. The result is some stop dreaming, and settle for what they have. The purpose of this chapter is to remind you of your dreams! When you are realigned with your dreams, you will be able to achieve what you want in life. What percentage of the population writes out their dreams and follows them for one year? I'll bet less than five percent.

The dream of having more things can be dangerous, especially when it supersedes the dream of having better relationships. I once heard my Dad say, "It's not what you make that counts, it's what you save." Dreams are like money in that way. If we don't invest in them, we won't see the returns. But who *hasn't* dreamed about having more money at some point in their life? Unfortunately, money is an illusion that many people mistake for a panacea.

If having more money is the *key*, why don't we pay more attention to how we use our money? For most of us, wealth is not made in a day, but over a period of time, as a result of following a plan. I see many people spend their money without understanding this, or the eventual impact on their families and life. They want to have money, but they always want new stuff. Why? We live in a materialistic world that is based on the concept that everything is disposable. Another reason is that many find it hard to define what enough is. The quest to get ahead in life drives people to spend. Usually when we are not satisfied with what we have, we are not satisfied with who we are. Dreams of money have driven many to do things we would not otherwise have done. Many people are driven to HAVE rather then to BE (balanced and at peace with oneself). We can have a great deal of wealth when we are at peace with who we are. Making dreams for stuff alone is not a way to true happiness. Money does not buy happiness, although it can buy opportunity. To create successful dreams we first need to focus on becoming the person we want to be. Then we can consider lifestyle. Being able to separate identity from lifestyle and to balance the two is important. There are too many people with a great deal of money who are not happy because they do not have themselves.

When I think about wealth, it is not only money. True wealth is a state of mind that encompasses gratitude and humility. I see it as knowing how to handle the money you have wisely, and having enough so as not to worry. Then you will find you have the time to do whatever you really want to do.

Reading *The Millionaire Next Door* (1996) had an impact on how I see money. It taught me that wealth is self-determined, and may not always have to do with money. Money is only one variable in the equation! I suggest that you read this book if you want some lessons on creating wealth.

My concern for us as a society is that we focus a great deal on wants, and not enough on needs. Too many people do not save for their families' futures. Ask any financial planner how many people have a strong financial plan. The people who do not have good plans still want money. The paradox is that many times they have more than enough money in their lives already. However, they are not using it to its full potential – they need plans to take care of their futures.

At the age of five, Sparkle Kitty learned that if you save your pennies, you will be able to save up for your future. In her case, her little piggy bank contains the money until she has enough to buy herself a toy or a treat. She does not understand credit yet, which is good when you think about it – she doesn't spend what she doesn't have.

For the most part, we all need credit, but many lose their dreams because of mismanagement of credit. They forget to self-evaluate. Self-management is important. For some, the problem comes from the individual's *wants* outweighing their *needs*. For example, if your TV is working, do you really need to buy a brand new $3,000 model because it has a new super high-tech picture tube?

The money dream is what many are chasing. However, whether it is money or something else we want, it all starts out as a dream. Once we make the dream, we need to work out the means to achieve it.

With money, you need a very specific means. How many have a means? Creating wealth is not hard. The key is to understand a basic principle known by all investors. It is the law of 72, which states that the percentage that your money is invested at, divided by 72, will tell you how long it will take to double. For example, if you invested $1000, and it averaged 10 percent return, you would have $2000 in exactly seven years and two months. The formula works – all people need to do is understand that there are no quick fixes, and their dreams can come true.

With any dream, you need a well-conceived plan of action. Luckily for us, there is already lots of information available on the means of getting almost anything. It is our responsibility to research and prepare the right formula.

As the process gets under way, our self-evaluation kicks in. It is important to guard against overdoing it – you don't need a nuclear bomb to open a stuck door. Some off us really go overboard when we hit roadblocks.

Pace yourself, and do only what is needed. Brian Tracy says many of us will need to work longer hours to realize our dreams. But he advises to work smarter – not harder. Time is only one measurement. Be aware of what you are doing, and its effect on other systems, like your family.

Do not fear failure. Invite it as a source of learning. Each failure brings you a step closer to your dream.

Make sure that you are not so gung-ho that your personal and professional ethics are compromised. Never hurt or take advantage of another person to get what you want. Always ensure you have *good intentions* where others are involved. This is a *code* we as humans must keep if we are to evolve, and help all human beings meet their needs.

Stick with the task. Don't give up! Think of the little engine that could. When things are tough, keep chugging along, keep your focus, and you will get there. Focus on the process, not the outcome, and you will get better results. You need to live in the present to make your future.

*Whatever the mind can conceive and believe, it can achieve. – Napoleon Hill*

I have a dream of having a successful coaching company. I want to offer a service that helps people improve who they are, at work and at home. The first part of my dream was that I needed to teach what I believed, so I wrote a lot of books. Then I needed to show my skills to others. To do this I had – and still have to – work with many people, to prove my coaching model. So the keys here are 1) making the dream; 2) taking action; 3) not being afraid of making mistakes; 4) believing! IBM founder Thomas

Watson never considered that his dream of building a successful company would not come true.

Being specific helps a lot. I remember playing golf one day, and telling myself that I needed more money. The intention of getting more money was on my mind. When I got to the fourth hole, I found eighty cents on the tee box. Yes, I got more money, but not what I really wanted. What is more, anyway? It is nothing unless we call it something. So define it, and be happy with it when you get it.

**Defining Your Dream**

1. What is your dream?
2. How do you know you want this dream?
3. Do you know how to obtain this dream?
4. What research do you need to do to obtain this dream?
5. Are you really prepared to do the work now for this dream?
6. When do you want to start this dream?
7. What are the steps and plan for this dream?
8. What are the consequences of obtaining this dream?
9. What are the benefits of this dream?
10. What are your timelines?

If you can set some of your answers down in writing, they will serve as powerful reminders. All dreams are attained one step at a time. For goal setting, I use the metaphor of a wave. Waves go in one direction with power and force, but they all have ups and downs. In life, we will have ups and downs, however, as long as we ride the waves of our specific goals, and look for the peaks, we will be able to turn our goals into reality.

One very important trait I know that will determine if you are going to realize your dreams is discipline. Of all the creatures in the animal kingdom, humans are the only ones who are not driven solely by genetic choice. A bird has no choice in winter but to fly south; a bear, to hibernate. They are genetically programmed. Humans have the choice to go south, east or west, and to sleep when they want to. We are blessed – or cursed, if you will – with choice. It is the paradox of our condition to be bound by free will!

Change takes time. Major change can be an accumulation of many tiny actions over a period of time. The *intensity* of the personality may influence the speed at which the change takes place. However, remember the lesson in the tortoise and hare fable. We can rush off with vigour, but if we don't have a plan and the necessary skills, it will only bring us more quickly to failure. I think we all need to be intense in life to a certain point, but our energy, conviction, and confidence need to be balanced, meaning we must be just as intense to please our children as we are to please our boss.

Discipline is an important element in starting and finishing dreams. We need self-discipline so we will continue to measure our progress and success. I see discipline, with its determination and sense of purpose, as the foundation of persistence.

When you invoke discipline, your dreams will meet success. What is success for you? I define success as:

**S**ecurity in what you have achieved.

**U**ltimate purpose defined.

**C**alm.

**C**onfidence that you will keep what you have earned.

**E**nthusiasm about each day of life.

**S**atisfaction with who you are and what you have, and knowing how to

**S**elf-correct without self-judging.

"Success will breed success." This is a common saying in the human development world. The Law of Attraction is as true for success as it is for quantum particles. It says that what we are is what we will attract to our world. When we are successful, we attract successful people. Success starts in the mind before it is ever physical.

Popular psychology guru Wayne Dyer argues that when we make a dream we need to be careful of what we ask for. He is quite literal in his belief that the universe does not judge – if our intentions are questionable, we may heap misery upon ourselves.

Scientist and philosopher Gary Zukav (1990) espouses the view that our intentions shape our reality. So beware of unconscious or conflicting intentions. They, too, may cause you or others harm.

Therefore, to be successful we must know our own hearts. Many of us live life through the eyes of others, and we make others more important than ourselves. We need to learn to balance our needs with those of others. When life presses our "hot buttons" (offends our sensitivities) it is nothing more than information. Others can do nothing except give us information, and it is our choice how we deal with it. Recognize your hot buttons – once you do, you'll be better able to cope with them. Have contingency plans for your dreams. Others don't kill our dreams – only we have that power. Try to anticipate some of the roadblocks you may encounter, and have clear detours in mind!

If you have a Plan B before you run into a problem, you will be less likely to fall off course. The road to quality living takes time and thought. Take time, and think about what you want in your life and if you are getting it. Well, are you? If you are not, I suggest you need to put this principle in motion. There is no better time than the present. The following ten points should get you thinking about what you want.

**Ten Tips to Help Your Dreams Come True**

1. Write down *all* of your ideas. Don't judge them; just write them.
2. If you have any limited beliefs about your potential, get rid of them. Hire a coach, take a course, and read self-learning books.
3. Keep your dreams running in your mind. What we focus on is what we will create. Remember what Napoleon Hill said, "What we focus on will expand."
4. Don't give up! You may need to redefine what is okay, but never give up. Ensure you celebrate the small victories on the way.
5. It's okay to have big dreams. Forget what others think. Dream, and be who you want to be. Set no boundaries! If Thomas Edison, Walt Disney, Alexander Graham Bell, Rosa Parks, John F. Kennedy, and so many others had set limits, where would we be? You are made of the same stuff, and have the same potential.
6. Support others in their dreams. It is important not to be jealous of others. There is plenty to go around. Believe in abundance! Help others climb their mountains – don't knock them off.
7. Empires take time to build – and lots of practice, patience, and persistence. Give yourself time.
8. Enjoy the process, and do not focus on the outcome. Inch by inch, life becomes a cinch.

# 9 The Power of Dreams

9. Flexibility and creativity are requisites for all of your dreams.
10. Be grateful for what you have. Do not fuss over what you do not have. Appreciate where you are *now*.

***In closing . . .***

We all have dreams as children. We all have dreams as adults. Sometimes we get too caught up in life to live them. Life is nothing more than what you want it to become. Once you have your dream, the most important step is the first step. Hold your course, and you will get to it. Do not give up on a dream if you have to adjust it. The only limit to a dream is the one we put on it. If you can't see it, you can't make it.

> Sparkle Kitty Coaching:
> I can do whatever I want; it is up to me. So can you!

## Sparkle Action

The activities listed below will help you study this chapter, and obtain the learning from it. The way to enhance your knowledge is by studying and self-reflection, and then practice.

1. On a scale of 1 (low) and 10 (high), how much are you already living this childmind principle today? _____

2. List three points from this chapter that may have had special significance for you:

    a) _____

    b) _____

    c) _____

3. How will this principle help you in each of the five *life balance* areas?
   In the space provided, be specific about each area:

   Health: _____

   Self: _____

   Relationships: _____

   Career: _____

   Money: _____

4. What is one dream you have?
   _____

   What is your action plan to attain it?
   _____

   List the steps here:
   _____
   _____
   _____

# Final Thoughts

I believe we all have but one life to live, and are all born with the skills to soar through it. Why we forget these skills isn't as important as remembering them. Knowing how wise a child can be, and how pure a new-born is, this shouldn't be impossible. Through daily practice and development of the nine childmind principles, we can recover as much of that wisdom and purity as we need. Below I have chosen one quote for each principle to stand as a reminder of its power.

**Nine Core Life Principles**

1. **Power of Love** – *One learns people through the heart, not the eyes or the intellect.* — Mark Twain

2. **Power of Courage** – *I have found that being honest is the best technique I can use. Right up front, tell people what you're trying to accomplish and what you're willing to sacrifice to accomplish it.* — Lee Iacocca

3. **Power of Fun** – *Develop interest in life as you see it; in people, things, literature, music – the world is so rich, simply throbbing with rich treasures, beautiful souls and interesting people. Forget yourself.* — Henry Miller

4. **Power of Hope** – *I will go anywhere as long as it is forward.*
   — David Livingston

5. **Power of Imagination** – *The maker of a sentence launches out into the infinite and builds a road into Chaos and old Night, and is followed by those who hear him with something of wild, creative delight.* — Ralph Waldo Emerson

6. **Power of Learning** – *Research shows that for jobs of all kinds, emotional intelligence is twice as important an ingredient of outstanding performance as cognitive ability and technical skill combined, and the higher you go in the organization, the more important these qualities are for success. When it comes to leadership, they are almost everything.* — Daniel Goleman

7. **Power of Faith** – *The spirit, the will to win, and the will to excel are the things that endure. These qualities are so much more important than the events that occur.* — Vince Lombardi

8. **Power of Family and Relationships** – *Since feeling is first / who pays any attention / to the syntax of things / will never wholly kiss you / wholly to be a fool / while Spring is in the world / my blood approves / and kisses are a better fate / than wisdom.* — e.e.cummings

9. **Power of Dreams** – *We judge ourselves by what we feel capable of doing; others judge us by what we have done.* — Henry Wadsworth Longfellow

My goal is to remind you of what's required for the life balance we all need. In time, we'll all get there. I see these principles as a key element for us all to become who we want to be. To build on these principles, I also teach what I call 11 Core Skills for Life.

**11 Core Skills for Life**

1. Self-assessing life position.
2. Determining personality type.
3. Defining communication models.
4. Defining core life values.
5. Defining life goals.
6. Defining your Life Plan.
7. Learning human behaviour.
8. Learning emotional intelligence.
9. Learning how we think.
10. Learning the Four Pillars of health.
11. Learning how to become your own coach.

These skills are found in two of my books, *My Personal Success Coach* and *An Employee's Survival Guide for the 21st Century*. Both books include a journal to help the individual practice the skills. The journals provide the necessary foundation to take full advantage of the information in the books.

Life is all we make of it, and it only takes effort to make it what we truly want.

Best wishes,

***Bill Howatt***

# Appendix A

# Your Childmind Score

I believe that everyone wants to do well. I also believe that childmind is a foundation for life balance. The following self-evaluation will show you how much you are using the childmind principles in your life today. This is not a psychological test – it is designed to help you measure how you are doing in each area, and to act promptly on areas that may need more focus.

Everybody needs to balance money, career, relationships, self, and health. *My Personal Success Coach* and *Dr. Bill's Life Coaching Manual* are tools to help people learn the skills that make life easier. The childmind principles, however, are the starting point.

Your answers to the questions below should reflect how your life really is, and what you are really doing – not what you think you should be doing.

The four choices are as follows:

**Very Untrue** – You totally disagree with this statement; it is not even close to what is happening in your life at present.

Untrue – The statement is not true to your life, however, you see that it is possible.

**True** – The statement is true for you, but not a major concern, although you spend some time on.

**Very True** – This statement is totally true, and you fully believe this is presently happening.

| Please check one answer that is applicable to you today. | | | | |
|---|---|---|---|---|
| **Power of Love** | Very Untrue 0 | Untrue 1 | True 3 | Very True 5 |
| 1. I have lots of love in my life today. | | | | |
| 2. I know how to love others. | | | | |
| 3. I am supportive of and have empathy for others. | | | | |
| 4. I like people, and like to help others. | | | | |
| 5. I work daily to show the people in my world I love them. | | | | |
| **Totals** | | | | |

| Please check one answer that is applicable to you today. | | | | |
|---|---|---|---|---|
| **Power of Courage** | Very Untrue 0 | Untrue 1 | True 3 | Very True 5 |
| 1. I am a person who can make decisions. | | | | |
| 2. I challenge what I do not agree with. | | | | |
| 3. I am confident in addressing my concerns. | | | | |
| 4. I can push myself through my fears. | | | | |
| 5. I express my opinions. | | | | |
| **Totals** | | | | |

| Please check one answer that is applicable to you today. | | | | |
|---|---|---|---|---|
| **Power of Fun** | Very Untrue 0 | Untrue 1 | True 3 | Very True 5 |
| 1. I spend time having fun in my life. | | | | |
| 2. I enjoy my fun time. | | | | |
| 3. I have hobbies to relax. | | | | |
| 4. I enjoy humour and laughter. | | | | |
| 5. I am a fun person. | | | | |
| **Totals** | | | | |

# Appendix A

| Please check one answer that is applicable to you today. | | | | |
|---|---|---|---|---|
| **Power of Hope** | Very Untrue 0 | Untrue 1 | True 3 | Very True 5 |
| 1. I am very positive towards others. | | | | |
| 2. I think good thoughts about others, and am non-judgmental. | | | | |
| 3. I believe that life is great, and I feel just great about my world. | | | | |
| 4. I am a positive person, and others know it. | | | | |
| 5. I am very optimistic about where I am going in the world, and know I will get there. | | | | |
| **Totals** | | | | |

| Please check one answer that is applicable to you today. | | | | |
|---|---|---|---|---|
| **Power of Creativity** | Very Untrue 0 | Untrue 1 | True 3 | Very True 5 |
| 1. I am very flexible. | | | | |
| 2. I am good at solving problems. | | | | |
| 3. I look for the opportunities in new beginnings, and accept change easily. | | | | |
| 4. I am what I say as a very creative person. | | | | |
| 5. I am a quick thinker, and can see options fast in life challenges. | | | | |
| **Totals** | | | | |

| Please check one answer that is applicable to you today. | | | | |
|---|---|---|---|---|
| **Power of Self-Esteem** | Very Untrue 0 | Untrue 1 | True 3 | Very True 5 |
| 1. I like who I am. | | | | |
| 2. I believe I can do what I want to in life. | | | | |
| 3. I am a confident person. | | | | |
| 4. I am proud of what I have done in my life. | | | | |
| 5. I am committed to liking who I am. | | | | |
| **Totals** | | | | |

| Please check one answer that is applicable to you today. | | | | |
|---|---|---|---|---|
| **Power of Learning** | Very Untrue 0 | Untrue 1 | True 3 | Very True 5 |
| 1. I like to learn. | | | | |
| 2. I take courses, just to learn more. | | | | |
| 3. I am aware of the importance of staying current. | | | | |
| 4. I am expanding my skills set. | | | | |
| 5. I read for pleasure and to expand my horizons. | | | | |
| Totals | | | | |

| Please check one answer that is applicable to you today. | | | | |
|---|---|---|---|---|
| **Power of Faith** | Very Untrue 0 | Untrue 1 | True 3 | Very True 5 |
| 1. I have a clearly defined faith. | | | | |
| 2. I practice my faith. | | | | |
| 3. I put stock in spirituality. | | | | |
| 4. I am active in my faith, and a student of it. | | | | |
| 5. I practice the principle of my faith daily. | | | | |
| Totals | | | | |

| Please check one answer that is applicable to you today. | | | | |
|---|---|---|---|---|
| **Power of Family** | Very Untrue 0 | Untrue 1 | True 3 | Very True 5 |
| 1. I have one loving relationship. | | | | |
| 2. I spend time with my family. | | | | |
| 3. I am a good parent or friend. | | | | |
| 4. I am a committed family member. | | | | |
| 5. I am satisfied with my family relationships. | | | | |
| Totals | | | | |

| Please check one answer that is applicable to you today. | | | | |
|---|---|---|---|---|
| **Power of Dreams and Goals** | Very Untrue 0 | Untrue 1 | True 3 | Very True 5 |
| 1. I have a clearly defined life plan. | | | | |
| 2. I write out and follow my life goals. | | | | |
| 3. I am presently taking action on my life dreams. | | | | |
| 4. I measure my goal success. | | | | |
| 5. I make adjustments so my dreams come true. | | | | |
| **Totals** | | | | |

## Score Chart

0-9  This is a principle that needs your immediate attention

10-19  This is a principle that you are actively living, but you need to spend more time and energy on this area.

20-25  This is a principle that is active and well in your life. Ensure you have a plan to keep it alive in your life.

# References

Bandura, A. (2001). *Self-Efficacy in changing societies, Ed.* Boston, MA: Cambridge.

Barke, J. (1992). *Paradigms.* New York, NY: Harper Collins.

Boorstein, S. (1998). *That's funny, you don't look buddhist.* New York, New York: Harper Collins.

Boorstein, S. (1998). *Siddhartha gautama buddha – the four noble truths.* New York, NY: Harper Collins.

Carlson, R. (1998). *Don't sweat the small stuff.* New York, NY: Hyperion.

Coloroso, B. (1994). *Kids are worth it.* Toronto, ON: Somerville House.

Cousins, N. (1991) *Anatomy of an illness.* New York, NY: Bantam.

Covey, S. (1989). *The seven habits of highly effective people.* New York, NY: Simon & Schuster.

Ellis, A. (1975). *A guide to rational living.* North Hollywood, CA: Wilshire.

Frankl, V.E. (1946). *Man's search for meaning.* New York, NY: Washington Square Press.

Geisel, T.S. (Dr. Seuss [pseud.] (1960). *Green eggs and ham.* New York, NY: Random House, Inc.

Glasser, W. (2000). *Choice theory.* New York, NY: Harper & Row.

Goleman, D. (1995). *Emotional intelligence.* New York, NY: Bantam.

Hawkins, D. (1995). *Power vs. force.* Arizona. Veritas Publications.

Hill, N. (1937). *Think and grow rich.* New York, NY: Fawcett Columbine.

Howatt, W.A. (1999). *A teacher's survival guide for the 21st century, second edition.* Kentville, NS: A Way With Words.

Howatt, W.A. (2000). *A relationship survival guide for the 21st century.* Kentville, NS: A Way With Words.

Howatt, W.A. (2000). *A parent's survival guide for the 21st century.* Kentville, NS: A Way With Words.

Howatt, W.A. (2000). *My personal success coach.* Kentville, NS: A Way With Words.

Howatt, W.A. (2000). *An employee's survival guide for the 21st century.* Kentville, NS: A Way With Words.

Kabat-Zinn, J. (1995). *Wherever you go, there you are.* New York, NY: Hyperion.

Massey, M. (1993). What You Are Is Where You Were When video series, Z107. Found on the world wide web: http://www.enterprisemedia.com/massey.html#anchor960561.

Peale, N.V. (1976). *The power of positive thinking.* New York, NY: Random House.

Peck, S. (1997). *The road less traveled.* New York, NY: Simon & Schuster

Seung Sahn (Dec. 1977). *Empty gate zen center.* Found on the world wide web: http://www.emptygatezen.com/

Stanley, T.J. and Danko, W.D. (1996). *The millionaire next door.* Marietta, GA: Longstreet.

Zukav, G. (1990). *Seat of the soul.* New York, NY: Fireside.